EXPOSING

THE SECRETS OF THE HEART

Dr. Theodore L. Dones

EXPOSING

THE SECRETS OF THE HEART

MESSENGERS OF FIRE MINISTRIES

Note: We use lowercase "s" for satan believing we do not acknowledge him, even to the degree of breaking the rules of grammar.

CONTACT US

Speaking Engagements, Conferences,

Crusades & Seminars

Email Us: teddones@messengersoffire.org

MESSENGERS OF FIRE MINISTRIES

WWW.FACEBOOK.COM/MESSENGERSOFFIREMINISTRIES

WWW.TWITTER.COM/APOSTLETED DONES

WWW.MESSENGERSOFFIRE.ORG

CONTENTS

FOREWORD By Dr. Maurice H. Sklar 7

FOREWORD By Dr. Larry Ollison 8

FOREWORD By Dr. Luis Lopez Jr. 9

FOREWORD By Dr. Bernie L. Wade 11

FOREWORD Apostle Warren Hunter 16

DEDICATION 17

ACKNOWLEDGMENTS 18

ENDORSEMENTS 19

ENDORSEMENTS 20

ENDORSEMENTS 21

INTRODUCTION 22

PART ONE EXPOSING THE MYSTERY 24

    CHAPTER ONE SECRETS OF THE HEART 26

    CHAPTER TWO REMAINING FREE 34

    CHAPTER THREE SIGNS AND WONDERS ARE NOT EVIDENCE OF FREEDOM 38

PART TWO UNDERSTANDING GOD AND HIS LOVE 42

    CHAPTER FOUR GOD'S LOVE 44

    CHAPTER FIVE THE UNVEILED WORD 48

    CHAPTER SIX LOVE'S ABILITY 52

    CHAPTER SEVEN LOVE GIVES WARNING 56

PART THREE MADE FREE, MADE EASY 64

    CHAPTER EIGHT PAY THE COST 66

    CHAPTER NINE YOU ARE FREE FROM THE LAW 70

PART FOUR CAPTURED AND PERFECTED 74

    CHAPTER TEN THE GOLD NUGGET 76

CHAPTER ELEVEN BE PERFECT..84

CHAPTER TWELVE YOUR SECRETS...91

CONCLUSION From the heart of the author 104

ABOUT THE AUTHOR...105

SCRIPTURE OUTLINE...107

ENDNOTES 119

APPENDIX A..120

FOREWORD
BY DR. MAURICE H. SKLAR

In this book, *Exposing the Secrets of the Heart*, Dr. Ted Dones shares revelations that cause hidden bondages to be exposed and removed permanently from our lives. So many of us struggle with addictions, secret habits of sin, emotional and mental strongholds, depression, anxiety, and other traumas from our past; there are healing and deliverance for you!

Through the process of grace, and our choice to come into the Light of God, we can be honest and transparent, and this allows the Holy Spirit to bring us to the very roots of our sins, addictions, and strongholds. Often, the real causes of our compulsive problems are not on the surface of our lives, but they stem from wounds, pain, and trauma from our past. Ted's book leads you on a journey into true freedom and lasting healing and deliverance by God's grace.

If you, dear readers, will open your hearts and let Yeshua (Jesus) minister to you, I believe that the Lord *will* set you free and empower you to live a holy, pure, and whole life in every area.

Victory is ours through our new life in our Messiah. Remember, "Greater is He that is in you than he that is in the world," and "...that good work that He has begun in you, he will also complete!"

I pray for the anointing of the Lord to break every yoke of bondage off of you as you read and study this powerful book!

Dr. Maurice H. Sklar
Maurice Sklar Ministries
Santa Maria, CA

FOREWORD

BY DR. LARRY OLLISON

There are many truths that when applied can be life-changing. To know the truth will set you free, and all truth originates with the Word of God. Dr. Theodore Dones, in his new and revealing book, *Exposing the Secrets of the Heart*, will take you step-by-step on a journey to living a life free from sin by revealing the truth of God's Word, and the final destination is freedom from bondage.

Through his years of proclaiming God's Word and his unique insight into the Scriptures, Dr. Theodore Dones will challenge you and guide you in your walk of love and understanding of God's grace. Read this book and continue to apply the principles contained in it and you will find freedom.

Dr. Larry Ollison
Larry Ollison Ministries
Osage Beach, MO

FOREWORD

BY DR. LUIS LOPEZ JR.

In the avenue of respect and honor, I will dare say that Dr. T.L. Dones has a keen eye on the heart of God regarding sin. Revelation has been poured out into this book for all to benefit, to distribute the understanding that there are men and women around the world today who are truly able to hear the cries of Christ's heart for His Church on earth, responding with true repentance and holiness and then writing it down on paper to express the character of The Lord for His people.

Surely, this book alongside the Bible will be a self-help teaching tool to assist the Body of Believers to overcome and experience real victory and joy in the Holy Ghost.

I am a firm believer that we do not battle to get the victory but battle from victory (We already won). In fact, when Dr. Dones speaks about matters and intents of the heart, we will be able to face ourselves with pure truth and honesty if we heed the tools he has placed in this manuscript, further helping the Church to be able to hold on firmly, catapulting us into a fresh relationship with the Lord.

I believe a fresh new fire will be released in these end-times for the people of God. We only have to be in the right position in our hearts to experience it. A refreshing is coming and coming quickly! We must be ready!

This reminds me of an important verse in the book of Proverbs, Chapter 28:13, where it states: *"He who covers his sin will not prosper, but whoever confesses and forsakes them will have mercy."* As the Church, in these last days, we need to think about what is really influencing us.

The Lord's Church must learn to allow the Spirit of Christ to germinate His love, compassion, and richness of mercy (which endures forever) to overtake them. I pray that each and every one of you will listen to a voice that God Himself has raised up in this hour, which must be heard. Apostle Ted Dones has mapped it out for you in this work of art.

Again, when Dr. Dones speaks about heart matters, he causes us to be able to face anything which comes our way. The pure truth will accelerate in your life if you decide for yourself to utilize these Life Points he has written, therefore assisting us to be able to hold on to the truth.

In conclusion, understand that you are loved and appreciated by The Father in heaven who has empowered us to become a peculiar people and a holy nation. Do not forget who you are in Christ, where you came from and what you've been taught. Holy Spirit is always with you to make sure that your spirit is in the right place in the eyes of Almighty God. This book will both encourage and give you the roadmap to succeed in this life.

Apostle Dr. Luis Lopez Jr.
Prophetess Dr. Michelle Lopez
Founders and President of:
Luis Lopez International Ministries
New Level Ministries International Church of Authority
Kingdom Fire International Church
International Connection of Apostles & Prophets
Rochester, NY

FOREWORD

BY DR. BERNIE L. WADE

The prophet Jeremiah said the *heart is deceitfully wicked, who can know it?* (Jeremiah 17:9). The answer to the riddle is *only* God. Some men desire or pretend to know the heart of man, but God has reserved the place of really knowing the heart of man for Himself.

I, the Lord, search the heart, I test the mind, even to give every man according to his ways, According to the fruit of his doings (Jeremiah 17:10).

As Biblical Christians, we know that mankind is wicked, and, without the Holy Spirit, there is no hope for humanity. More than a generation ago, a preacher addressed a large congregation with this question:

"Tonight, if I could take the three secret sins of your heart and reveal them up on the wall at the front of the auditorium for all to see, how many of you would stay in the building?"

This is quite a word picture. No doubt you can imagine the discomfort of those in the congregation. If he had started calling people out, claiming he was about to reveal their sins, some would have left the building.

Yet this preacher was only trying to find a way to get past the walls that we put up and touch the heartstrings of those in his hearing. It is unlikely that most of us would be comfortable having such a public demonstration reveal those things that are in our hearts. However, those 'secret sins' are only hidden from men.

They are certainly not hidden from God. Secret sins affect every relationship: a husband and wife; a mother or father and their children;

church leaders and the people they serve; and the list goes on. It is an endless list.

In a conservative southern church, the pastor's wife found pornography on her husband's computer. After confronting him with the evidence, he admitted downloading the images off the internet and even using the computer in his study, which was located in the church itself. Somehow, he had separated his ongoing sexual sin from his responsibilities and duties as a man of God. Often, we seem to think that that which is hidden from others does not affect us – but it does.

The availability of modern communication has brought us not to more sin but merely to easier and more readily available access to sin. What once was something that men had to leave their homes in order to indulge can now be delivered to their desktop. satan is clever.

In another Bible-believing church, a Christian businessman sought investment capital from other Christian individuals and businesses. He promised to invest the money in new Christian enterprises and promised a high rate of return on their money.

Alas, there was no new enterprise, and there was no return on their money. He had embezzled hundreds of thousands of dollars from his fellow Christians. He was charged by civil authorities and jailed. I wish that this was not a common theme, but it has been repeated more than we realize.

A nice Christian family joined a local church by letter of recommendation from another city. Kenneth and Barbie had five wonderful little boys ranging from two to twelve years of age. Barbie sang a special song in the church and played the keyboard. Kenneth was a Bible scholar and had taught Bible study at their former church.

However, Kenneth and Barbie had a terrible secret. Kenneth had a terrible temper that caused him to abuse his family both physically and emotionally.

No one in the church had any idea until Barbie took her boys and left to return to her hometown. Kenneth followed her back in an attempt to reconcile. In short, there are often no happy endings to these hidden 'heart secrets' - but there are always victims.

Proverbs 28:13 says. *"He that covereth his sins shall not prosper: but whoso confesseth and forsaketh them shall have mercy."* The word "covereth" means *to hide or conceal*. The word "prosper" means *to advance succeed, make progress*. There are professing Christians in almost every church who believe that they are prospering in spite of hidden, secret sins; they have convinced themselves that their sin is condoned by God. But there is no real success when you carry the baggage of secret sin in your life.

Secret sins are not new. Since the beginning of time and the very first sin, man has sought to hide or keep his sin a secret from God.

Here are some examples:

Hiding Disobedience

After Adam and Eve had disobeyed God by eating from the tree, "*they heard the sound of the Lord God walking in the garden, and the man and his wife hid themselves from the presence of the Lord*" (Genesis 3:8-11).

Jonah fled from the presence of the Lord (Jonah 1:3). *But Jonah ran away to Tarshish to escape from the presence of the LORD [and his duty as His prophet]. He went down to Joppa and found a ship going to Tarshish [the most remote of the Phoenician trading cities]. So he paid the fare and went down into the ship to go with them to Tarshish away from the presence of the LORD.*

Hiding Idolatry

God said to the prophet Ezekiel, "*Son of man, do you see what the elders of the house of Israel are committing in the dark, each man in the room of his carved images? For they say, 'The Lord does not see us.'*" (Ezekiel 8:12)

Hiding Murder

After Cain killed his brother Abel, God asked him, "*Where is Abel your brother?*" And he said, "*I do not know. Am I my brother's keeper?*" (Genesis 4:9)

Hiding Stealing

After the battle of Jericho, Achan said to Joshua, "*I have sinned against the Lord, when I saw the spoil I coveted them and took them; and they are concealed in the earth inside my tent.*" (Joshua 7:16-26)

Hiding Adultery

After David's adultery with Bathsheba (and the murder of her husband), Nathan the prophet of God told David, *"Why have you despised the word of the Lord by doing evil in His sight? ... You did it secretly."* (2 Samuel 12:9, 12)

Hiding by Lying

Ananias and Sapphira lied to Peter about the price of some property they sold. Peter said to them, *"Why is it that you have conceived this deed in your heart? You have not lied to men, but to God."* (Acts 5:1- 7)

Here are several things you should consider about secret sins:

First, do not let yourself be deceived. *"Whoever makes a practice of sinning is of the devil ... No one born of God makes a practice of sinning, for God's seed abides in him, and he cannot keep on sinning because he has been born of God."* (1 John 3:8, 9) while not completely free from sin, the heart of the true believer has been transformed, and they cannot live in a pattern of continual sexual sin.

Second, the exhortation is to *"... confess your sins to one another and pray for one another, that you may be healed."* (James 5:16)

Third, fear is not a virtue. Yes, exposure will be costly, but right now you are dying on the inside. It may not feel like dying right now, but you are, you are slowly killing yourself, your spouse, your family, and your congregation.

Fourth, if secret sexual sin has severe consequences, it is worth dealing with before the devastation occurs. Obvious examples come to mind to get help before your Internet browsing history is discovered and shared; before the prostitute turns into an undercover policewoman and you are arrested for soliciting; before you contract an STD; or before you are publicly exposed, humiliating yourself, your spouse, your family, and your congregation.

Fifth, it will come out. God is never mocked. *"Note then the kindness and the severity of God: severity toward those who have fallen, but God's kindness to you, provided you continue in his kindness."* (Romans 11:22)

Sixth, getting caught shatters trust and honesty in marriage, embarrasses your spouse, and makes reconciliation more difficult.

Seventh, there is hope. It begins with facing the truth. It is never just a struggle with your thought life; like all sexual sin, it is evil. If there is an old-self to put off, there must be a new-self to put on; that is the gospel.

My friend, Dr. Ted Dones has written this powerful book dealing with these issues: *Exposing the Secret Sins of the Heart*. It is a book that is well worth the reading and will make a positive impact on your life. It is time to live in freedom. Jesus Christ shed His blood not only so that we could have life, but that we could have it more abundantly.

I know Ted, and his lovely wife, Janet. I find them to be wholly committed to the work of the Lord! Not perfect by any means (none of us are), but good Godly people. In the old West, crossing rivers was a very treacherous endeavor. Having people to help you with crossing the river was very valuable. In fact, your life depended upon having that help.

The old timers would say it like this: "*That is someone that you can ride the river with.*" This was a high compliment to the person, their character, their experience, their level-headedness, and their life.

Life is like one of those rivers. There are often very treacherous things that we encounter. Having people that you can trust on the journey is crucial. I have found Ted and Janet Dones to be people that I can *ride the river'* with, and I am honored to count them among my friends.

Read this book; pass it on to a friend. It may well be the best thing you could do for them. We *all* struggle with sin. Man was born in sin and shaped in iniquity. Those of us who are filled with the Holy Spirit have been delivered from that sin nature!

Do not allow yourself to be entangled again with the things of the world. If you have - repent! Tomorrow will be a new day! Get help. That is why Apostle Ted Dones wrote this book. Like Apostle Paul, we must continue to "die daily" shedding those sins of the heart from our lives. Blessings!

Dr. Bernie L. Wade, President
International Circle of Faith
Louisville, KY

FOREWORD

APOSTLE WARREN HUNTER

In Hebrews 4 verse 12 the word dividing is a Greek word Merismos but when one looks deeper it implies probing of that innermost resources of the total human personality I love what F.F.Bruce says in his book, (new international commentary on the New Testament,) "The word of God probes the innermost recesses of our spiritual being and brings the subconscious motives to light". Ted Dones has done this and more in showing how the convicting power of the Holy Spirit in the heart must be restored!

Apostolic Revivalist Warren Hunter
Sword Ministries International
Branson, Mo

DEDICATION

First and foremost, I want to dedicate this book to the Lord Jesus Christ. Secondly, I would like to dedicate this book to my beautiful wife, Janet, who has stood beside me through thick and thin. I am grateful for all her many hours of prayer intercessions for me as I labored in the word for many days and weeks, so this message from the Lord could be clearly presented to the people of God. I believe with this message they will be delivered from the bondage of satan.

I would also like to thank my precious daughter who gave up years of being with her parents as we traveled across the United States so that we could help bring liberty and freedom to God's people in Jesus name!

Dr. Theodore Dones

ACKNOWLEDGMENTS

I would like to thank my beautiful wife Janet for her loving, thoughtful and helpful suggestions as I sought God during the writing of this book, and for her commitment which has meant more to me than words could ever say.

I also would like to personally thank all my friends and acquaintances (which are too many to write here - *smile*), including those who took the time to read the rough manuscript of this book and keep me in prayer as I was writing it.

Thank you so much!

Dr. Theodore Dones

ENDORSEMENTS

Dr. Ted Dones has been inspired by the Holy Spirit to reveal the entrapments of men's hearts to bring liberty to the captive in the name of Jesus. Dr. Dones is bold and spot on to get to the root causes people today. He is a personal friend that has inspired my life personally. Expect an explosive revival fire to birth transformation in your heart and soul through the revelation that has been revealed in this book.

Evangelist Stan T. Lovins II
Sandlot Ministries International
Revival for the True Jesus Christ &
MY HOPE with Billy Graham
(Area Coordinator) Victory Training
Indianapolis, IN

ENDORSEMENTS

I have known Dr. Ted and his lovely wife, Janet, for many years now. They are in hot pursuit to bring all people to the awareness of God's love for them. As you set yourself to pursue the principles in this book, you too will become empowered with true confidence, not only to be established in Grace but to be able to help others know their Creator better and find His true plan and purpose for them as you become better established in your own.

Prophet Larry Green
Still Waters International Ministries
Springs Walnut Shade, MO

ENDORSEMENTS

The word of God says in John 8:32 *"And you shall know the truth, and the truth will make you free."* Dr. Ted Dones challenges us through his new book, *Exposing the Secrets of the Heart,* to examine ourselves to reveal the secrets deep within that would keep us from being healed, delivered, and made free. If there ever was a book that calls for complete honesty with oneself, this book does. As you are honest with yourself, chains will be broken, yokes will be destroyed, and you will be made free by the power of The Risen Savior.

Dr. Ruth Wilson
Shekinah Glory International Ministries
Louisville, KY

INTRODUCTION

I n this hour, many professing believers are falling into the practice of sin. Sadly, this unprofessed sin not only secretly inhabits their heart, but it also begins to rule it as well.

When the choice to harden your heart and remain in sin is made, eventually you will no longer be able to hear God, nor discern the things of God. As a result, you will begin to listen to the wrong voice and, in confusion, you will not be able to determine the correct one.

Mercifully, there are Godly answers to hidden heart sins and their devastating effects. These answers come from God's Holy Word, the ministering of the Holy Spirit, and with the help found within *Exposing the Secrets of the Heart.*

Exposing the Secrets of the Heart is a life-changing, must-read book! It is not only for those who are struggling with hidden sin, but is for all those who want to know how to open their hearts to God and live overcoming lives.

When I minister these Biblical truths, many people are fully healed from sickness and delivered from drugs and sin. You too no longer have to be bound and can claim your freedom and victory today in Jesus Name!

Sadly, there are many people today who are busying themselves with religious good works and, as a consequence, are running far away from engaging themselves in what they should be working on; which is *Exposing the Secrets of the Heart.* As a result, they are repeatedly battling broken hearts and failures, and are finding themselves struggling with sexual sin, drug addiction, financial lack, and ungodly habits.

If you are in a continuous battle with the same challenges in your life (marriage, family, health, finances), and you have never been able to overcome them, then *Exposing the Secrets of the Heart is* the key that will help catapult you into glorious freedom*!*

Now is the time to exam your heart. If you are struggling with hidden sin, truly desire to be healed, and you do not understand why you cannot attain physical or emotional healing, *Exposing the Secrets of the Heart* should be your heart's cry.

As you read this powerful, dynamic book, and follow its Biblical principles, you will never again suffer from hopelessness, discouragement, and defeat.

From these pages, you will learn how to see your heart as God sees it. Also, you will learn how to let go of the hidden sin which seeks to keep you back from enjoying healing, freedom, peace, and victory in your life.

Let's journey together! Exposing the Secrets of the Heart will place you on the right path so that you can discern between the truth and the error that may reside within your heart.

Today is your day to walk towards the absolute freedom to be all that God has called you to be so that you can fulfill everything that He has predestined you to achieve.

"The secrets of his heart will be revealed, and as a result he will fall facedown and worship God, proclaiming, "God is really among you."

(1 Corinthians 14:25 CSB)

PART ONE

EXPOSING THE MYSTERY

"For where your treasure is, there your heart [your wishes, your desires; that on which your life centers] will be also. The eye is the lamp of the body; so if your eye is clear [spiritually perceptive], your whole body will be full of light [benefiting from God's precepts]. But if your eye is bad [spiritually blind], your whole body will be full of darkness [devoid of God's precepts]. So if the [very] light inside you [your inner self, your heart, your conscience] is darkness, how great and terrible is that darkness! No one can serve two masters; for either he will hate the one and love the other, or he will be devoted to the one and despise the other. You cannot serve God and mammon [money, possessions, fame, status, or whatever is valued more than the Lord]."

Matthew 6:21-24 AMP

CHAPTER ONE
SECRETS OF THE HEART

You can be released, forever, from all of the things that are tormenting and imprisoning you! Does that statement thrill your heart? Does it allow you to have hope when, at times, there seems to be very little hope? I will state it again...*there is a way to obtaining Holy Spirit filled freedom in every area of your life...and **truly** keeping it forever.*

Let me quickly, and in Jesus Name, eradicate the lie that is seeking to destroy you; which whispers that you will be forever shackled to torment, fear, sin, unforgiveness, or whatever *it* is. If having true and everlasting freedom is a desire in your heart, then **YES** there is hope; tremendous and wonderful hope!

In order to successfully achieve, and forever abide in, this freedom, I will guide you (step by step) on how you can sincerely examine your own heart. In addition, with God's Holy Word, I will teach you how to be free from the lies and chains of sin and deception.

Let us begin with two questions that I want you to meditate on deeply:

Question 1

What secrets are you hiding in your heart?

Question 2

Is there anything keeping you from receiving the fullness of the love that God has for you?

I posed these questions to you at the beginning of our journey together in order for the Holy Spirit to begin His Work within your heart. For it is within the heart that we learn whether we love God more than we love our secrets.

When we examine the secrets that lie within the heart, it is important to know what the meaning of the word *secret* is in the original languages. In the Greek, we find the words *kroop-tos* or *kroop-to* which means: *concealed by covering; hide.* The Hebrew word is *tah-al-oom-maw*, and it means: *Thing that is hidden; to veil from sight or conceal.*

Accordingly, we see here that a secret is *concealed* or *hidden.* Therefore, to expose hidden secrets, another important question we must consider is *"What do we love more than we love God?"* This is relevant because whatever we love more than we love God keeps us from His Presence, and also from His blessings.

When we love something more than God, it can overpower us and can become our hidden *sin life.* The word *overpower* means: *to overcome by superior force; to defeat.* As you can now begin to see and understand, the result of having a hidden sin life is bondage.

IDENTITY OF SIN UNVEILED

Let me give you another way to identify hidden heart sin, Christian author Charles Finney is noted for sharing a quote by his grandmother; *"anything is sin which impedes or hinders God in life."*

If you are willing, we will continue to journey together in order to expose what you have hidden deep within your heart so that the truth will make you free.

Let us begin...

As children of God, we cannot love Heaven's Light and the devil's darkness at the same time. The Bible warns us of the danger of loving evil:

"Their sentence is based on this fact: that the Light from heaven came into the world, but they loved the darkness more than the Light, for their deeds were evil. They hated the heavenly Light because they wanted to sin in the darkness. They turn away from that Light for fear their sins would be exposed, and they would be punished. But those doing right came gladly to the Light to let everyone see that they were doing what God wants them to." (John 3:19-21 TLB)

Therefore, sin must be exposed and brought to the Light so that we can walk in the Light. Without the Light, darkness keeps one blind.

"Sin lurks deep in the hearts of the wicked, forever urging them on to evil deeds. They have no fear of God to hold them back. Instead, in their conceit, they think they can hide their evil deeds and not get caught. Everything they say is crooked and deceitful; they are no longer wise and good. They lie awake at night to hatch their evil plots, instead of planning how to keep away from wrong." (Psalm 36:1-4 TLB)

When we have done wicked things in the dark, we try to hide them out of a sense of shame and the fear of punishment. In other words, we do not want anyone to know what we have done, or what we are currently doing. As a consequence, this fear binds us in a prison of torment and seeks to keep us from being exposed to the Light.

In essence, Light will expose hidden secrets. The Light of the Gospel is sent into the world to show people their transgressions, and to reveal evil deeds. This is why when we have secret sin we hate the Light of the Gospel.

Christ is the Light, and He is hated because those who plan to continue practicing wickedness hate the Light. That is to say that there are some who practice sin and willfully barricade themselves in a prison of darkness because they love their sin more than they love Him.

The Light will expose hidden secrets, and those who do not come to the Light have a secret loathing for the Light. However, those with upright hearts do not fear the Light, they embrace it.

"This is the message which we have heard from Him and declare to you, that God is light, and in Him is no darkness at all. If we say that we have fellowship with Him, and walk in darkness, we lie, and do not practice the truth: But if we walk in the light as He is in the light, we have fellowship with one another, and the blood of Jesus Christ His Son cleanses us from all sin." (1 John 1:5-7 NKJV).

Jesus came with a message of the Love of God, and it was that very love which revealed their sin. He exposed and confronted it boldly wherever He went. Notice that Jesus spoke the Word to those around Him and He was the one that uncovered their sin:

"He who sins is of the devil, for the devil sinned from the beginning. For this purpose, the Son of God was manifested, that He might destroy the works of the devil."(1 John 3:8 NKJV)

Unfortunately, most people do not know how to become free. The problem is that the Church tells people they are sinners, but it does not teach them how to become, and remain, free.

The children of God who have been set free are called to reveal the way to freedom through Jesus Christ and Him crucified. Exposing the deeds of darkness to those trapped in the bondage of sin is what God's Love and Light compels us to do.

In giving your heart to Jesus, we recognize that He came that we might have life (a life which brings hope and freedom) and to have it more abundantly. When we are living within the abundant life found only in Him, He commands us to go out to the ends of the earth manifesting the Light and Love of God.

When you study the Bible, you will find one constant theme from Genesis to Revelation; our Father God wants His children free! Know this; *God is in the business of setting His people free.*

It is exciting to learn that Jesus is certain that, as children of God, we are capable of being victorious and conquering overcomers. In the book of Revelation, when speaking to the Seven Churches, Jesus told them the same thing that He is telling us today; to overcome.

In the Greek language, the word *overcome* is *nikao*, pronounced as *nik-as-o* meaning *to conquer, subdue, prevail, and get victory* . In the Hebrew language, the Word *overcome* is ya^ko^l, pronounced *yaw-kole* - meaning *"to be able, attain, endure, and have power."*

The Church is the body of Christ. As the Church, *we are expected* to overcome. Unless we overcome, we will never inherit the Kingdom of God.

What is it that we must do to overcome? We must overcome sin and willfully doing whatever feels good. Unfortunately, instead of overcoming our sin and disobedience, we obstinately refuse to deal with the veiled and deceptive issues within our hearts.

The only way to be able to overcome sin is by the power of the Holy Spirit. David said:

"Create in me a clean heart, O God, and renew a steadfast spirit within me. Do not cast me away from Your presence, and do not take Your Holy Spirit from me. Restore to me the joy of Your salvation and uphold me with Your generous Spirit. Then I will teach transgressors Your ways, and sinners shall be converted to You." (Psalms 51:10-13 NKJV)

The Power and The Blood of the Lord Jesus Christ brings you into the place where you are totally free and healed. It is the place in which Father God dwells. It is the Holy of Holies.

Many people believe that living a good life and doing good things will get them into the presence of God. This is not true. People with this type of mindset have missed it. The truth is, we will never enter into the Holy of Holies through anything that we do. There is only one way, and that way is through The Blood of Jesus Christ.

"Therefore, brothers, since we have this confidence to enter the Most Holy Place by the blood of Jesus, by a new and living way opened for us through the curtain, that is, his body, and since we have a great priest over the house of God, let us draw near to God with a sincere heart and with the full assurance that faith brings, having our hearts sprinkled to cleanse us from a guilty conscience and having our bodies washed with pure water." (Hebrews 10:19-22 NIV)

SPIRITUAL FREEDOM

My wife and I have a heart's desire and a profound mission for our lives; to help others become free from tradition and religiosity. Since many have learned, and are currently operating in this particular way of thinking, breaking these mindsets is often difficult. However, the Lord has given me the tools to assist anyone who is looking for real freedom spiritually. The Word of God says, *"... where the Spirit of the Lord is, there is liberty."* (2 Corinthians 3:17 NIV)

Therefore, *it is the power of God that cleanses our hearts.* Living an overcoming life of freedom, and staying in His presence, is God's will for you! Come to Jesus! Mean it with all of your heart and surrender all to Him.

"Because if you acknowledge and confess with your lips that Jesus is Lord and in your heart believe (adhere to, trust in, and rely on the truth) that God raised Him from the dead, you will be saved. For with the heart a person believes (adheres to, trusts in, and relies on Christ) and so is justified (declared righteous, acceptable to God), and with the mouth he confesses (declares openly and speaks out freely his faith) and confirms [his] salvation." (Romans 10:9-10 AMPC)

The Blood of Jesus has already paid the price for every ungodly hidden sin resonating within you. When you come to Jesus with sincerity, and with a hunger to be cleansed of all sin, He will also cleanse you of all guilt. Furthermore, He will give you a fresh fire and a deep passion to live for Him - and that passion will never run out. As a matter a fact, the more you read His Word, and the more you engage in fasting, your passion for Him will increase.

Transformation

Sanctification is not a word that we hear much of these days. Nonetheless, today, more than ever, it is very much needed in the Body of Christ. In simple terms, the word sanctification is *the process of becoming holy* or *to be set apart for sacred use.*

Sanctification is the evidence of salvation, and the two can never be separated. Sanctification is the Holy Spirit's Divine procedure of making you holy unto God and filled with the Truth of Christ.

Sanctification is work done by the Spirit and is why both salvation and sanctification work together. In other words, once you are saved, the Holy Spirit begins the process of transformation in your life; heart, mind, and actions.

This is how we know that we have been saved and that the Spirit of God now dwells within us. God would never leave us in our mess. Once He comes and inhabits our hearts and lives, His Spirit begins the *good work* of setting us apart unto Himself; making us separate from this world and likening us into the image of His Son Christ Jesus.

It is truly a beautiful action from the Lord and is evidence of His great love for each one of us. For no one who truly loves you would ever leave you in hopelessness, pain, and in the grip of eternal damnation. Praise

God! For God's Love and Grace through Christ, and the process of sanctification, the effects of sin and death are purged from us.

"But we are bound to give thanks to God always for you, brethren beloved by the Lord, because God from the beginning chose you for salvation through sanctification by the Spirit and belief in the truth"

(2 Thessalonians 2:13 NKJV)

Spiritual Nugget 1

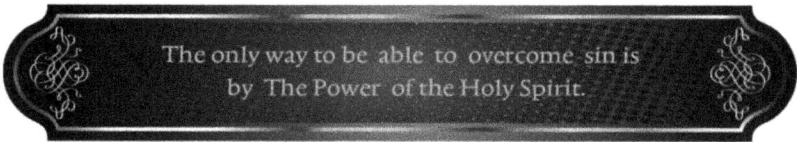

The only way to be able to overcome sin is by The Power of the Holy Spirit.

"And they overcame him by the blood of the Lamb and by the word of their testimony, and they loved not their lives unto the death."

Revelation 12:11 NKJV

CHAPTER TWO
REMAINING FREE

The way to overcome temptation and sin is by The Blood of the Lamb, and by sharing the testimony of what God has done for you. These two vital keys will reveal the hidden things within your heart in order to bring you freedom and empower you to remain free.

In order to remain free, you cannot go back to your old ways of doing things. You must choose life and follow Christ. Jesus told His disciples

"Enter through the narrow gate; for wide is the gate and spacious and broad is the way that leads away to destruction, and many are those who are entering through it. But the gate is narrow (contracted by pressure), and the way is straitened and compressed that leads away to life, and few are those who find it." (Matthew 7:13-14 AMPC)

The way into the Holy of Holies is narrow. God's Way is the only way that we will make it. Therefore, by accepting the finished work of Jesus and His shed Blood, we come to understand and recognize that He is the only Way because Jesus is *"The Way, the Truth, and the Life."* (John 14:6 NKJV)

We each have challenges in our lives that we must overcome; various issues and struggles that we battle one way or another. Unfortunately, there are times when we would rather stay in our bondage than admit to anyone that we have a problem and need help. Yet, each of us are to die daily to our selfish desires and to live unto God. Let me show how we choose the darkness over freedom:

"But now, after that, you have known God, or rather are known by God, how is it that you turn again to the weak and beggarly elements, to which you desire again to be in bondage?" (Galatians 4:9 NKJV)

The word *element* in the Greek language is *stoykhion* – meaning: *"basic fundamental principles."*

Paul was asking the Galatians h*ow can you allow yourselves to be brought back into the law, that thing which has no power to cleanse your souls.*

The Galatians had received Christ. They were delivered from the bondage of the law, yet they were allowing themselves to be drawn back into it by outside influences. Consequently, we see here that although they had received Christ, they were still babes in Christ and had not learned how to overcome the temptations that came their way. Paul admonished them several times:

"Dear brothers, I have been talking to you as though you were still just babies in Christian life, who are not following the Lord, but your own desires; I cannot talk to you as I would to healthy Christians, who are filled with the Spirit. I have had to feed you with milk and not with solid food because you couldn't digest anything stronger. And even now you still have to be fed with milk.

For you are still only baby Christians, controlled by your own desires, not God's. When you are jealous of one another and divide up into quarreling groups, doesn't that prove you are still babies, wanting your own way? In fact, you are acting like people who do not belong to the Lord at all." (I Corinthians 3:1-3 TLB)

AVOID AND OVERCOME CORRUPT AFFECTIONS

Moreover, the Galatians had received some of the first principles of Christianity, but they had not grown to maturity. Again, they were babies. The Bible tells us about the danger of not maturing to exercise one's faith: *"... faith by itself, if it does not have works, is dead."* (James 2:17 NKJV)

The people in the Corinthian church had Paul himself ministering to them, yet they still quarreled amongst themselves and acted like babies. They were taught by someone who had a revelation of Christ like no other, and yet they still bickered. They did not have an understanding of how to overcome sin and bondage. They let sin command their lives.

It is clear that those in bondage are under the command (and control) of corrupt affections. In order to become free, you must put your Godly knowledge into practice so that the power of God will be released in you.

The hidden sin in our hearts must be brought out and exposed. The Bible teaches us how to avoid letting sin rule us and taking us into bondage. This is the purpose of our testimonies. It is one of the safeguards we have been given to getting and remaining free.

The Scripture tells us, *"...they overcame him by the blood of the Lamb, and by the word of their testimony..."* (Revelation 12:11 KJV)

Spiritual Nugget 2

> In order to become free, you must put to work what you know so that the power of God will be released in you.

"Not everyone who says to Me, 'Lord, Lord,' shall enter the kingdom of heaven, but he who does the will of My Father in heaven. Many will say to Me in that day, 'Lord, Lord, have we not prophesied in Your name, cast out demons in Your name, and done many wonders in Your name?' And then I will declare to them, 'I never knew you; depart from Me, you who practice lawlessness!'

Matthew 7:21-23 NKJV

CHAPTER THREE
SIGNS AND WONDERS ARE NOT
EVIDENCE OF FREEDOM

Many people today are deceived in believing that if they are operating in the gifts of the Spirit with signs and wonders that it proves that they are free from sin. This is absolutely unbiblical.

God gave me the revelation that you can go to hell flowing in every gift in the Bible. In other words, just because you have a revelation of who Christ is does not mean you will go to Heaven. Notice that the Bible says the gifts and calling of God are without repentance:

"For God's gifts and His call are irrevocable. [He never withdraws them when once they are given, and He does not change His mind about those to whom He gives His grace or to whom He sends His call]." (Romans 11:29 AMPC)

As children of God, we are commanded to go forth into the entire world and teach others how to overcome sin. Each of us must live out our walk every day – just as Enoch, Elijah, and Moses also were commanded - even Jesus had to walk out His faith on a daily basis:

"And Jesus being full of the Holy Ghost returned from Jordan, and was led by the Spirit into the wilderness, being forty days tempted of the devil. And in those days, He did eat nothing: and when they were ended, He afterward hungered. (Luke 4:1-2 KJV)

"And Jesus answered and said to him, "It has said, 'You shall not tempt the Lord your God.' " Now when the devil had ended every temptation, he departed from Him until an opportune time." (Luke 4: 12-13 NKJV)

OVERCOMING SIN

Let us take another look at this verse by reading it from another translation: *"When the devil had finished all this tempting, he left Him until an opportune time."* (Luke 4:13 NIV)

This scripture tells us that Jesus had to overcome the temptation of sin just as we do.

The walk of faith is not different, but is the same for everyone. Therefore, if Jesus had to overcome sin, we are no exception. One day, we will stand before the judgment seat of God to be judged for how we reacted to the temptations of sin during our walk on this earth.

Pay close attention to this verse that shows how God is not a respecter of persons:

"And if ye call on him as Father, who without respect of persons judgeth according to each man's work, pass the time of your sojourning in fear." (1 Peter 1:17 ASV)

Let me clarify what we just read. God will render unto every man according to his deeds. The time of our sojourning (or life) here on earth is to be passed in fear of God. Holy confidence in God as a Father, and reverent fear of Him as a judge, are very consistent throughout Scripture.

The judgment of God will be passed on without favoritism according to each man's work. The word *work* in Greek is *ergo*, which means *to toil [as an effort or occupation]; deed, labor, doing.* We will be judged for our works during our walk on this earth.

"Not everyone who says to Me, "Lord, Lord, shall enter the kingdom of heaven, but he who does the will of My Father in heaven. Many will say to Me in that day, Lord, Lord, have we not prophesied in Your name, cast out demons in Your name? And then I will declare to them, I never knew you; depart from Me, you that practice lawlessness!" (Matthew 7:21-23 NKJV)

Those who have sown unrighteousness in their lives, or who chose rituals and religion over having a true relationship with the Father, will receive tribulation and wrath.

"Now he who plants and he who waters are one, and each will one will receive his own reward according to his own labor." (1 Corinthians 3:8 NKJV)

God gives honor, glory, and eternal life to those who do His will. Let me share with you two Scriptures which will show you the eternal reward that we will receive when we obey God and overcome temptation and sin.

First, Paul defines the eternal reward for him and every believer that finished the course and did not quit:

"I have fought the good fight, I have finished the course, I have kept the faith: henceforth there is laid up for me the crown of righteousness, which the Lord, the righteous Judge, shall give me at that day, and not to me only, but also to all them that have loved his appearing." (2 Timothy 4:7-8 ASV)

Second, the Scripture tells us that an overcomer will receive a crown of life.

"Blessed is the man that endures temptation; for when he has been approved, he will receive the crown of life, which the Lord has promised to those who love Him." (James 1:12 NKJV)

ETERNAL REWARDS

To sum it up, performing signs and wonders does not prove we are sinless and that we will go to heaven. You do not make it to heaven based on your gifts. Instead, it is daily walking in the truth of God's light (which clearly exposes our deeds), and the eternal rewards we receive will be based on what we have done in God.

"But he who does the truth comes to the light, that his deeds may be clearly seen, that they have been done in God." (John 3:21 NKJV)

There are many passages in the Bible that declare the numerous rewards given to an obedient believer in Christ who does the will of the Father. Moreover, we must not give away something that is real and substantial. If anything, we must run to it. Jesus is that person we can all run to.

Jesus made a Huge Promise of returning for His people in the end-times. Therefore, if you have anything secretly residing in your heart holding you back from prospering, my urgent advice to us is to go before the Throne of Grace and confess it to Him. Or, go to someone you trust and to whom you are accountable and take care of it, immediately.

Messengers of Fire Ministries does not desire that anyone should perish and end up left behind.

Our prayer is that you will enter into the Kingdom of God, which is righteousness, peace and joy in the Holy Spirit which is evidence of your eternal security.

Spiritual Nugget 3

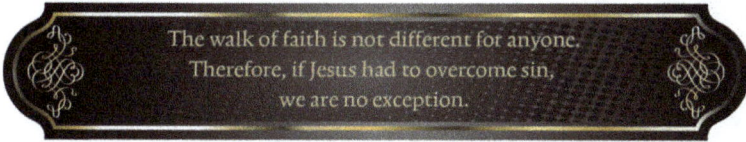

> The walk of faith is not different for anyone. Therefore, if Jesus had to overcome sin, we are no exception.

PART TWO

UNDERSTANDING GOD AND HIS LOVE

"But God demonstrates His own love toward us, in that while we were still sinners, Christ died for us"

Romans 5:8 NKJV

CHAPTER FOUR
GOD'S LOVE

God's Love forever changes our focus on life. When you draw near to Christ, and open up the secrets of your heart to Him, He will draw near to you with His Love. To know if people understand God's Love, I ask them this question: *What were you saved from?*

Most people tell me they were saved from hell, but that cannot be the right answer because hell was not made for us. Hell was prepared for the devil and his demons.

On the contrary, when we truly understand God's Love, we will no longer focus on His wrath, but we will see His Love:

"Much more then, being now justified by his blood, shall we be saved from the wrath of God through him." (Romans 5:9 ASV)

The crucifixion and resurrection of Jesus Christ saved us from the wrath of God. We incurred this wrath because, as a race, we chose to do *our own thing* instead of abiding in His Love.

"For when we were still without strength, in due time Christ died for the ungodly. For scarcely for a righteous man will one die, yet perhaps for a good man, someone would even dare to die. But God demonstrated His own love toward us, in that, while we were still sinners, Christ died for us." (Romans 5:6-8 NKJV)

"But if our unrighteousness thus establishes and exhibits the righteousness of God, what shall we say? That God is unjust and wrong to inflict His wrath upon us [Jews]? I speak in a [purely] human way." (Romans 3:5 AMPC)

Thank God that He loves us! The word *commend* is the Greek word *sunistao*, which means *to introduce, to stand with*. When God sent His Son, He introduced us to His Love. Let us take another look at a previous passage, but read it from another translation:

"But God demonstrates his own love for us ... (when) Christ died for us ..." (Romans 5:8 NIV, *word in parenthesis was* added.)

Do you know how much God loves you? Take the time to meditate on what the Apostle John has written

"For God so loved the world that he gave His only begotten Son, that whoever believes in Him should not perish, but have everlasting life. For God did not send His Son into the world to condemn the world, but that the world through Him might be saved. He who believes on Him is not condemned; but he who does not believe is condemned already because he has not believed in the name of the only begotten Son of God." (John 3:16-18 NKJV)

"Or do you have no regard for the wealth of His kindness and tolerance and patience [in withholding His wrath]? Are you [actually] unaware or ignorant [of the fact] that God's kindness leads you to repentance [that is, to change your inner self, your old way of thinking – seek His purpose for your life]?" (Romans 2:4 AMP)

"Now hope does not disappoint, because the love of God has been poured out in our hearts by the Holy Ghost, who was given to us." (Romans 5:5 NKJV)

FOLLOW THE LEADER

Unless a person allows the Holy Spirit to lead their heart into the Love of God, they will never step foot inside of a church. The Love of God leads men to repentance, and the Love of God will draw the heart of a man.

In today's society, most people think that if they want to find God, they can find Him in a church. The truth is that you will find God in a church that welcomes the Holy Spirit. When a person feels the drawing of the Holy Spirit, they will look for God until they find Him.

"Draw near to God and He will draw near to you." (James 4:8 NKJV).

"Come close to God [with a contrite heart], and He will come close to you. Wash your hands, you sinners; and purify your [unfaithful] hearts, you double-minded [people]." James 4:8 (AMP)

The Bible tells us how to draw close to God

"let us approach [God] with a true and sincere heart in unqualified assurance of faith, having had our hearts sprinkled clean from an evil conscience, and our bodies washed with pure water. (Hebrews 10:22 APM)

If God had not shown you that you needed Him, you would not have come to know Him.
"And He was saying, "This is the reason why I have told you that no one can come to Me unless it has been granted him [that is unless he is enabled to do so] by the Father." (John 6:65 AMP)

I thank God for His love. If I had not felt the Holy Spirit's drawing, and responded by drawing near to Him, I would not know Him right now.
The Holy Spirit transforms us to be like Christ
"But we all, with unveiled face, beholding as in a mirror the glory of the Lord, are being transformed into the same image from glory to glory, just as by the Spirit of the Lord." (2 Corinthians 3:18 NKJV)

As Love perfects Himself in me, and I die to my selfish desires, I am learning that by His Grace I become more like Him. This is available to you as well. It is freely available to all who will draw near to God; to all who will open up the hidden secrets of their hearts to Him.

"I have been crucified with Christ; it is no longer I who live, but Christ lives in me; and the life which I now live in the flesh I live by faith in the Son of God, who loved me and gave Himself for me." (Galatians 2:20 NKJV)

Spiritual Nugget 4

When you draw near to Christ and open up the secrets of your heart to Him, He will draw near to you with His love.

"but just as it is written [in Scripture], "Things which the eye has not seen and the ear has not heard, And which have not entered the heart of man, All that God has prepared for those who love Him [who hold Him in affectionate reverence, who obey Him, and who gratefully recognize the benefits that He has bestowed]." For God has unveiled them and revealed them to us through the [Holy] Spirit; for the Spirit searches all things [diligently], even [sounding and measuring] the [profound] depths of God [the divine counsels and things far beyond human understanding]."

1 Corinthians 2:9-10 AMP

CHAPTER FIVE
THE UNVEILED WORD

When we were first born again we each received the Spirit of God. One of the many blessings which came from receiving the Holy Spirit was that we could know, and recognize, the things that have been freely given to us by Him.

Beforehand, when you had the spirit of the world, there was a veil over your heart and mind which kept you from understanding God's Word and knowing the things of God. As you continue reading this book, I want to encourage you to meditate on God's unveiled word until it is hidden in your heart. This is how to keep your heart free from hidden secrets. Just like a dear friend of mine, Dr. Luis Lopez Jr., always says,

"As long as you remain under The Shadow of the Almighty, which is mentioned in Psalms chapter 91, you will be hidden from satan himself. It's only when you make yourself available to sinful desires that he sees you standing outside The Shadow."

Therefore, we entrust the fact that the Sword of the Spirit (The WORD) needs to be hidden within our spirit so that it may protect us when the enemy reveals himself. Because of this, we are more than able to place the enemy into a position that is hard for him (and his minions) to come out of. Unfortunately, since we have indulged too much in the flesh, if the Word is not hidden within us, it can cause us to fall.

WORD REVELATION

One day, the Lord told me to write down the word *F-L-E-S-H*. He said to me, *"Write it down and then look at the word. What do you see? Now erase the "H" and read the word backwards. Now, what do you see?" "You will see the word "S-E-L-F."*

Then the Lord said to me, *"Remember the pictures of dots that have hidden pictures within them? Remember when you looked at them that you couldn't see anything but dots? But, when someone came up and pointed out the pictures to you, then you were able to see the picture. Such is the Word of God."*

God unfolds His Word to us and makes it clear.

"But, on the contrary, as the Scripture says, What eye has not seen, and ear has not heard and has not entered into the heart of man, [all that] God has prepared (made and keeps ready) for those who love Him [who hold Him in affectionate reverence, promptly obeying Him and gratefully recognizing the benefits He has bestowed]. Yet to us God has unveiled and revealed them by and through His Spirit, for the [Holy] Spirit searches diligently, exploring and examining everything, even sounding the profound and bottomless things of God [the divine counsels and things hidden and beyond man's scrutiny].

For what person perceives (knows and understands) what passes through a man's thoughts except the man's own spirit within him? Just so no one discerns (comes to know and comprehend) the thoughts of God except the Spirit of God. Now we have not received the spirit [that belongs to] the world, but the [Holy] Spirit Who is from God, [given to us] that we might realize and comprehend and appreciate the gifts [of divine favor and blessing so freely and lavishly] bestowed on us by God." (I Corinthians 2:9-12 AMPC)

One day God asked me, *"Teddy, do you know why I wrote the Bible?"* I gave Him a bunch of dumb answers. Then He said to me, *"I wrote the Bible so that I could find Myself in you. You search the Scriptures for salvation, but the Scriptures reveal Christ."*

The Lord then asked me, *"Do you know why I placed My Word within you?"* I pondered this question, and then He answered: *"I put My Word within the darkest place I could find, and that was your heart."* You see, He already knew the hidden secrets of my heart.

"In the beginning was the Word, and the Word was with God, and the Word was God. He was in the beginning with God. All things were made by Him, and without Him, nothing was made that was made. In Him was life, and the life was the light of men. And the light shines in darkness and the darkness did not comprehend it." (John 1:1-5 NKJV)

By standing firm on the above Verse, we use it to solidify our freedom in Jesus. We meditate on the Word of God until it is hidden in our hearts, replacing the deadly secrets.

Spiritual Nugget 5

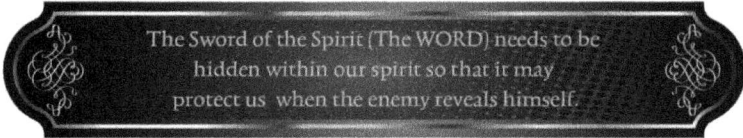

The Sword of the Spirit (The WORD) needs to be hidden within our spirit so that it may protect us when the enemy reveals himself.

"For His divine power has bestowed upon us all things that [are requisite and suited] to life and godliness, through the [full, personal] knowledge of Him Who called us by and to His own glory and excellence (virtue). By means of these He has bestowed on us His precious and exceedingly great promises, so that through them you may escape [by flight] from the moral decay (rottenness and corruption) that is in the world because of covetousness (lust and greed) and become sharers (partakers) of the divine nature."

II Peter 1:3-4 AMPC

CHAPTER SIX

LOVE'S ABILITY

God's absolute, and limitless, ability to love us keeps us free from sin. One of the significant things that I am learning is that most of God's people do not have a true revelation about His Love, or of His Love for them. The Revelation of His Love, and His Truths, comes from time spent in His Word, in His presence, and in learning to know Him. God gives you a revelation of Who He Is so that you will pour out unto others what He has given to you.

One day I was in a car driving down the road, and I kept hearing a clanging noise from the front left wheel. I just ignored it. Finally, I said, *"Man, that noise is just annoying."* I heard the Lord say, *"That's you.* "I asked, *"What?" God answered me, "That's you. You are not anything but a clanging symbol. You have tons of revelation, but where is the love? Where is the love in you that I have for My people?"*

The Bible says

"If I [can] speak in the tongues of men and [even] of angels, but have not love (that reasoning, intentional, spiritual devotion such as is inspired by God's love for and in us), I am only a noisy gong or a clanging cymbal. And if I have prophetic powers (the gift of interpreting the divine will and purpose), and understand all the secret truths and mysteries and possess all knowledge, and if I have [sufficient] faith so that I can remove mountains, but have not love (God's love in me) I am nothing (a useless nobody). Even if I dole out all that I have [to the poor in providing] food, and if I surrender my body to be burned or in order that I may glory, but have not love (God's love in me), I gain nothing." (1 Corinthians 13:1-3 AMPC)

MIND YOUR RESOURCES

I cannot love anyone out of my own resources, but I can love others through Jesus. So, I cried out, *"God, perfect Your love in me. I want Father God's Agape Love because I can't love Your people unless You put Your love in me. I can't get sin out of me unless You take it out of me."*

In order for you and I to be able to receive the love of God, and overcome sin, we must be delivered from self. The Bible says that God is the one who delivers us:

"Now see that I, even I, am He, And there is no God besides Me; I kill, and I make alive; I wound and I heal; Nor is there any who can deliver from My hand" (Deuteronomy 32:39 NKJV).

In short, no one can deliver but God. If it were possible to be set free without God, we would not need Jesus. The law was righteous, good, and holy, but it could not remove sin. Nor could it bring redemption or cleanse our hearts. The power of 'Love's Ability' is that Christ has made you free.

"For the law of the Spirit of life [which is] in Christ Jesus [the law of our new being] has set you free from the law of sin and of death. For what the Law could not do [that is, overcome sin and remove its penalty, its power] being weakened by the flesh [man's nature without the Holy Spirit], God did: He sent His own Son in the likeness of sinful man as an offering for sin.

And He condemned sin in the flesh [subdued it and overcame it in the person of His own Son], so that the [righteous and just] requirement of the Law might be fulfilled in us who do not live our lives in the ways of the flesh [guided by worldliness and our sinful nature], but [live our lives] in the ways of the Spirit [guided by His power]." (Romans 8:2-4 AMP)

That is why God's redemption plan was sending His own Son Jesus to earth because Jesus' shed Blood would remove our sin and bring us to redemption. We need Jesus. The shed Blood of Jesus Christ gave us all power in heaven and on earth. Most of us cannot comprehend how amazing that truth is - He gave **US ALL** authority in heaven and earth!

"For His divine power has bestowed upon us all things that [are requisite and suited] to life and godliness, through the [full, personal] knowledge of Him Who called us by and to His own glory and excellence (virtue). By

means of these He has bestowed on us His precious and exceedingly great promises, so that through them you may escape [by flight] from the moral decay (rottenness and corruption) that is in the world because of covetousness (lust and greed) and become sharers (partakers) of the divine nature." II Peter 1:3-4 AMPC)

These Scriptures sum it all up. Everything we need has been given to us through Love's Ability. Remember, He will fulfill all things in their season, and our part is to simply allow ourselves to be guided by the Holy Spirit.

Spiritual Nugget 6

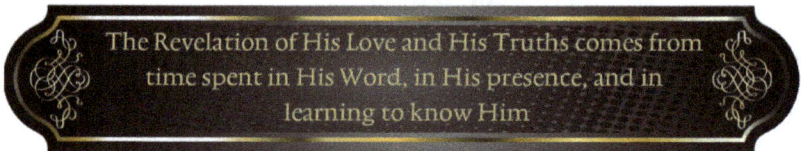

The Revelation of His Love and His Truths comes from time spent in His Word, in His presence, and in learning to know Him

"But God clearly shows and proves His own love for us, by the fact that while we were still sinners, Christ died for us. Therefore, since we have now been justified [declared free of the guilt of sin] by His blood, [how much more certain is it that] we will be saved from the wrath of God through Him."

Romans 5:8-9 AMP

CHAPTER SEVEN

LOVE GIVES WARNING

God, through His Holy Word, gives us a warning so that we would remain free from His Wrath. To help us understand how God's Love purifies our hearts, and warns us against His wrath, I will present several questions for you to answer by looking into God's Word.

To begin, we need to know what causes people to suffer God's wrath. Throughout God's Word, He makes a critical and fundamental point very clear; sin and rejection of His Son produces his wrath.

Take another look at what God said in the verse for this chapter.

"But God shows and clearly proves His [own] love for us by the fact that while we were still sinners, Christ (the Messiah, the Anointed One) died for us. Therefore, since we are now justified (acquitted, made righteous, and brought into right relationship with God) by Christ's blood, how much more [certain is it that] we shall be saved by Him from the indignation and wrath of God." (Romans 5:8-9 AMPC)

If God saves us from His wrath and sin produces wrath, then I am saved from sin.

This brings us to our *first* question:

What is sin?

God calls sin *missing the mark.* God sets the mark. Our actions are a picture of what is going on inside of us. The acts of sin draw God's wrath and that is why we must completely surrender ourselves to God.

"Therefore, put to death your members which are upon the earth: fornication, uncleanness, passion, evil desire, and covetousness, which is idolatry"(Colossians 3:5 NKJV).

"For we have spent enough of our past lifetime in doing the will of the Gentiles - when we walked in licentiousness, lusts, drunkenness, revelries, drinking parties, and abominable idolatries." (I Peter 4:3 NKJV)

As we review the above scripture, we need to ask ourselves the *second* question:

Do these things bring the wrath of God upon us?

Paul tells us that they do. The Bible explains it this way:

"Because of these things the wrath of God is coming on the children of disobedience." (Colossians 3:6 NKJV).

So, the Bible is clear; God sets us free from His wrath. Nevertheless, God's wrath came upon us as children of disobedience.

However, since we were not created as children of disobedience, God made a redemption plan for us. God did not intend for us to be vessels of wrath. His purpose in showing us His wrath was to reveal His power to us. In setting us free from His wrath, the Bible goes on to say; we become vessels of mercy prepared for glory.

"What if God, although fully intending to show [the awfulness of] His wrath and to make known His power and authority, has tolerated with much patience the vessels (objects) of [His] anger which are ripe for destruction? And [what if] He thus purposes to make known and show the wealth of His glory in [dealing with] the vessels (objects) of His mercy which He has prepared beforehand for glory."(Romans 9: 22-23 AMPC)

In other words, God warns us of His Wrath for one purpose; so that we may know that Christ in us is the hope of glory.

"To whom God was pleased to make known how great for the Gentiles are the riches of the glory of this mystery, which is Christ within and among you, the Hope of [realizing the] glory. Him we preach and proclaim, warning and admonishing everyone and instructing everyone in all wisdom (comprehensive insight into the ways and purposes of God), that we may present every person mature (full-grown, fully initiated, complete, and perfect) in Christ (the Anointed One)." (Colossians 1:27-28 AMPC)

For this reason, we are to preach Christ and Him crucified so that we may be presented to God on that day as perfect men and women.

Christ is coming back for a pure church; one that is without spot or wrinkle.

"that He might sanctify and cleanse it with the washing of water by the word, that He might present her to Himself a glorious church, not having spot, or wrinkle or any such thing, but that she should be holy and without blemish." (Ephesians 5:26-27 NKJV)

We bring the wrath of God upon ourselves when we refuse to cleanse our temples. A good example of this is found in II Chronicles. Hezekiah went into the temple to open it. The first thing he did was clean it out. As a result of the filthiness of the temple, the wrath of God came down. Let's read how that happened:

"In the first year of his reign, in the first month, he opened the doors of the house of the Lord and repaired them. Then he brought in the priests and the Levites, and gathered them together in the East Square, and said unto them: "Hear me, you Levites! Now sanctify yourselves, sanctify the house of the Lord God of your fathers, and carry forth the rubbish from the holy place. For our fathers have trespassed and done evil in the eyes of the Lord our God; they have forsaken Him, have turned their faces away from the habitation of the Lord, and turned their backs on Him.

They have also shut up the doors of the vestibule, put out the lamps, and have not burned incense or offered burnt offerings in the Holy Place to the God of Israel. Therefore, the wrath of the Lord fell upon Judah and Jerusalem, and He has given them up to trouble, to astonishment, and to jeering, as you see with your eyes." (II Chronicles 29:3-8 NKJV, emphasis added.)

This leads to my third question:

Where is the temple of God today?

"Do you not know and understand that you [the church Ekklesia] are the temple of God and that the Spirit of God dwells [permanently] in you [collectively and individually]? If anyone destroys the temple of God [corrupting it with false doctrine], God will destroy the destroyer; for the temple of God is holy (sacred), and that is what you are." (1 Corinthians 3:16-17 AMP)

"Run away from sexual immorality [in any form, whether thought or behavior, whether visual or written]. Every other sin that a man commits is outside the body, but the one who is sexually immoral sins against his own body. Do you not know that your body is a temple of the Holy Spirit who is within you, whom you have [received as a gift] from God and that you are not your own [property]?" (1 Corinthians 6: 18 -19 AMP)

THE TEMPLE AND THE MIND

My point is this; we are the temple of God; we are to possess our temple in honor and sanctification, and only then will we see the glory of God!

We cannot stand in the glory of the Lord, covered in sin. After Adam sinned, God could no longer come to him as He once did. God was forced to drive Adam out of the garden because if He had come to Adam during his sin, Adam would have died. God's wrath came upon man because of Adam's sin. If God came and found us currently in sin, it would kill us.

There are nights, as I lay in bed, God comes into my room and says, *"I AM GOD,"* and I immediately think, "I am filthy." He pours His Holy Presence over me and the fear of God washes over me. I now understand what Moses meant when he said:

"Moses said to the people, "Do not be afraid; for God has come in order to test you, and in order that the fear of Him [that is, a profound reverence for Him] will remain with you, so that you do not sin." Exodus 20:20 (AMP)

I wake up at times with trembling in my heart knowing that His return is getting close. I pray: "God do whatever you have to do in me to make me ready."

During a visit at a pastor's home (while I was resting in the Lord), I began reading the book *The House of the Lord* by Francis Frangipane. During my reading, God Himself ministered to me through its pages. It was as if I were reading a love letter from Him to me. While I was having this amazing love experience with God, I remembered something wonderful that my wife had previously shared with me. She had told me that she had dreamt that I was reading a love letter. It was then that I realized that this book was the love letter that my wife had dreamt about beforehand. I began to weep.

Francis Frangipane made the following statement in his book *Cleansing the Holy Place...*

"Within every Christian, there is a secret place, a sanctuary that we must prepare for the Lord. (You are that sanctuary.) This holy place is unlike the holy of Holies in Jewish temples. Not until this place is clean will the Lord dwell in us in the fullness of His Spirit."

It was then that I understood the price to have God's Glory dwell within us. It is not until each one of us is pure will we entirely become a house of the Lord. When I read that, I said, *"Dwell in me, God. Set up Your tabernacle in me. Whatever keeps me from you, I do not want it."* When we let God dwell within us, we will be able to set captives free.

The devil wants to keep God's people bound in sin, and if we remain in bondage by sin then God cannot come and dwell in the Holy place within us. The devil also tells people that they are unworthy of God's love. He tells them that God will not forgive them of their sin because they are unclean. The devil is a liar! He is a murderer, thief and a destroyer and his only purpose is to steal, kill, and destroy us.

The thief comes only in order to steal and kill and destroy. I came that they may have and enjoy life, and have it in abundance (to the full, till it overflows)." (John 10:10 AMP)

Saving Grace

Within the churches that I minister, I deal with uncleanliness in many of its forms: fornication, adultery, homosexuality, and pornography to name a few.

"idolatry, sorcery, enmity, strife, jealousy, anger (ill temper), selfishness, divisions (dissensions), party spirit (factions, sects with peculiar opinions, heresies), Envy, drunkenness, carousing, and the like. I warn you beforehand, just as I did previously, that those who do such things shall not inherit the kingdom of God." (Galatians 5:20-21 AMP)

Do you know what happens when God reveals the bondage within us? We get set free. He mercifully reveals the bondages that we are trapped in so that we can be loosed from our sin.

Yet, God knew that after we had cried out to Jesus for redemption that there would still be work that needed to be done. He also knew that accomplishing this work was impossible on our own; that we could not do it without Him. This is the reason that we must share our testimony; telling of the wonderful things that God has done for us. In addition, we should also share our sin one to another, so that *we may be healed.*

The book of James states, "*Come close to God, and He will come close to you. [Recognize that you are] sinners, get your soiled hands clean; [realize that you have been disloyal] wavering individuals with divided interests, and purify your hearts [of your spiritual adultery]."* (James 4:8 AMPC)

This leads to my *fourth* questions:

> *How do we cleanse our hands and purify our hearts and remain free of sin?*

We can find the answer in this passage,

"How can a young man cleanse his way? By taking heed according to Your word. With my whole heart I have sought You; Oh, let me not wander from Your commandments! Your word I have hidden in mine heart, That I might not sin against You. Blessed art You, O Lord! Teach me Your statutes." (Psalm 119:9-12 NKJV)

This scripture makes it clear exactly how to keep our hearts pure and free from sin. As we meditate upon the Word of God, the Word cleanses us.

"This Book of the Law shall not depart out of your mouth, but you shall meditate on it day and night, that you may observe and do according to all that is written in it. For then you shall make your way prosperous, and then you shall deal wisely and have good success." (Joshua 1:8 NKJV)

"But his delight and desire are in the law of the Lord, and on His law (the precepts, the instructions, the teachings of God) he habitually meditates (ponders and studies) by day and by night." (Psalms 1:2 NKJV)

As we hide the Word in our hearts, the Word builds up a resistance to sin within us. The more time we spend in the Word, the less we desire to sin.

The more we desire to know God, the better life becomes. This is called renewing of our mind.

Truly, when we sincerely fall in love with God, we will allow Him to deal with the sin in our hearts. One of the benefits of God removing sin from our hearts is that He will remove all idols from it and from our lives; for anything that we love more than God is considered idolatry.

For example, there was a time in my life that I loved my wife more than I loved God. She used to be an idol in my heart, but over time (as God continued to perfect His Love within me) I realized that she never loved me as Jesus loved me. She is unable to love me like Jesus is capable and willing to love me. No one can love another person as unconditionally, as deeply, and as perfectly as Jesus can.

After tasting Heaven (which is Almighty God Himself), I have learned not to allow anything or anyone to keep me from Him. If I begin to detect any sin within my life, I immediately cast down the thoughts that try to take hold of me.

In summary, I have made it my life's goal to learn to die to sin (and to my own self) and live to God.

I believe with all of my heart that when we, as the Body of Christ, begin to live the way that I have just written (according to the Word of the Lord), we can come to know the Will and Purity of the knowledge of Christ.

We can then begin to have divine manifestations in our lives and will also experience true transformation through Him.

Paul said it this way: *"But whatever former things I had that might have been gains to me, I have come to consider as [one combined] loss for Christ's sake. Yes, furthermore, I count everything as loss compared to the possession of the priceless privilege (the overwhelming preciousness, the surpassing worth, and supreme advantage) of knowing Christ Jesus my Lord and of progressively becoming more deeply and intimately acquainted with Him [of perceiving and recognizing and understanding Him more fully and clearly].*

For His sake I have lost everything and consider it all to be mere rubbish (refuse, dregs), in order that I may win (gain) Christ (the Anointed One), And that I may [actually] be found and known as in Him, not having any [self-achieved] righteousness that can be called my own, based on my obedience to the Law's demands (ritualistic uprightness and supposed right standing with God thus acquired), but possessing that [genuine righteousness] which comes through faith in Christ (the Anointed One), the [truly] right standing with God, which comes from God by [saving] faith.

[For my determined purpose is] that I may know Him [that I may progressively become more deeply and intimately acquainted with Him, perceiving and recognizing and understanding the wonders of His Person more strongly and more clearly], and that I may in that same way come to know the power outflowing from His resurrection which it exerts over believers], and that I may so share His sufferings as to be continually transformed [in spirit into His likeness even] to His death, [in the hope] That if possible I may attain to the [spiritual and moral] resurrection [that lifts me] out from among the dead [even while in the body]." (Philippians 3:7-11 AMPC)

Spiritual Nugget 7

God's "love warning" will keep us free as long as we do God's will and not our own

PART THREE

MADE FREE, MADE EASY

"When He had called the people to Himself, with His disciples also, He said to them, "Whoever desires to come after Me, let him deny himself, and take up his cross, and follow Me. For whoever desires to save his life will lose it, but whoever loses his life for My sake and the gospel's, will save it. For what will it profit a man if he gains the whole world, and loses his own soul? Or what shall a man give in exchange for his soul?"

Mark 8:34-37 NKJV

CHAPTER EIGHT
PAY THE COST

Did you know that the entire book of First Peter talks about dying to your flesh? Paul said, *"To live is Christ, to die is gain."* To die daily to the flesh {your mind, your will, and your emotions} is to gain spiritual things. In other words, the more we die to the flesh, the more of the knowledge of the glory of God we will have. You must cleanse your body, the temple so that the glory can come in. As I said before, the glory of God cannot reside in an unclean temple.

Do you want the glory? Are you willing to pay the price for the glory of God? Keep in mind; it will cost you everything. Let us read these scriptures from Mark Chapter 8 (Amplified) and study the cost verse by verse.

Verse 34

"...Jesus called the crowd together with His disciples, and said to them, "If anyone wishes to follow Me [as My disciple], he must deny himself [set aside selfish interests], and take up his cross [expressing a willingness to endure whatever may come] and follow Me [believing in Me, conforming to My example in living and, if need be, suffering or perhaps dying because of faith in Me]."

Verse 35

"For whoever wishes to save his life [in this world] will [eventually] lose it [through death], but whoever loses his life [in this world] for My sake and the gospel's will save it [from the consequences of sin and separation from God]."

Verse 36

"For what does it benefit a man to gain the whole world [with all its pleasures], and forfeit his soul?"

Verse 37

"For what will a man give in exchange for his soul and eternal life [in God's kingdom]?

King David bought the threshing floor to offer a sacrifice to God. The owner of the threshing floor was willing to give it to King David, but King David said, *"I will not offer anything to God that costs me nothing."*

This does not make sense to the natural and carnal mind. If we lose something, how do we gain something more from that loss? Why would we give up all that we are holding on to from within our hearts? The answer to this is absolutely critical and key; when we release what is precious to us, and give it to God, we gain everything. Look at what Paul said to the Galatians concerning this same matter:

"Do not be deceived, God is not mocked [He will not allow Himself to be ridiculed, nor treated with contempt nor allow His precepts to be scornfully set aside]; for whatever a man sows, this and this only is what he will reap. For the one who sows to his flesh [his sinful capacity, his worldliness, his disgraceful impulses] will reap from the flesh ruin and destruction, but the one who sows to the Spirit will from the Spirit reap eternal life." (Galatians 6:7-8 AMP)

HARD WORK MADE EASY

Did you understand that? You mean that we receive life everlasting? The answer is without a single doubt Yes! When we die to the flesh, we gain life everlasting here and now. And I know Beloved, it is not always easy to walk after the Spirit daily, but it is possible.

The Lord's standards are really high, and because they are high there may be times when we tend to talk ourselves out of doing holy things. We say in our minds, *"I am not Jesus!"* No, we are not Jesus. However, we can wholeheartedly thank Him for His sacrifice in our place. Why? Due to the fact that we were not able to fulfill the LAW that the Lord God created for humanity.

We needed someone to do it for us; One Who is completely without sin, thus bringing forth true redemption and freedom. Messiah's

(Moschiach) loving {and absolutely wonderful} act of sacrifice for you and I resulted in LIFE forevermore being made available to all who would receive Him.

The price has been paid for each of us to become the beneficiaries of the Lord Jesus Christs' finished work. What an awesome thing that He has done for all humanity. In addition, oone of the glorious fruits of this is that payment was made in full so that we can now walk peacefully and confidently within His grace and mercy. Praise God in the Highest!

Consequently, we live within God's Grace without taking advantage of Christ and the Grace that He so mercifully has gifted us with because we love Him.

There are many who, upon hearing the Good News of what God has done for all, accept it wholeheartedly. However, since we are born not in Grace but in sin, there are many who also hear the Gospel of Grace and do not accept or receive it - which genuinely grieves my heart.

Yet, I remember that there was a time before accepting Jesus as my Lord and Savior that I could count myself amongst the ones who did not immediately accept it either. But I tell you the truth, the Holy Spirit is never too far away to reach the lost.

Spiritual Nugget 8

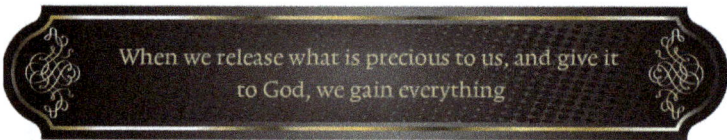

When we release what is precious to us, and give it to God, we gain everything

"For I through the law died to the law that I might live to God."

Galatians 2:19 NKJV

CHAPTER NINE
YOU ARE FREE FROM THE LAW

Jesus Christ has made us completely free from the law. In this chapter, I am going to ask you a few questions which will show you several ways to understand what God's Word has to say about being free from the law.

Paul said, *"For I through the law died to the law that I might live to God."* (Galatians 2:19 NKJV)

This verse introduces us to our next set of questions in which the Word of God will provide the answers.

Question 1:

How did Paul die to the law?

"that the righteousness requirement of the law might be fulfilled in us who do not walk according to the flesh but according to the Spirit." (Romans 8:4 NKJV)

In other words, we understand that it is *a spiritual walk*. The righteousness of the law is fulfilled when we allow the love of God to be poured into our hearts by the Spirit. Mercifully, as the love of God grows within us, the law is fulfilled.

Question 2:

"Is the righteous requirement of the Ten Commandments, or the law, relevant today?"

I answer with a resounding, "Yes, it is!" Why?

Paul said we die to the law by obeying the law, but not in our own strength but by the power of the Holy Spirit. Jesus said, *"Do not think that I came to do away with or undo the Law [of Moses] or the [writings of the] Prophets; I did not come to destroy but to fulfill."* (Matthew 5:17 AMP)

"Where is boasting then? It is excluded. By what law? Of works? No, but by the law of faith. Therefore, we conclude that a man is justified by faith apart from the deeds of the law. Or is He the God of the Jews only? Is He not also the God of the Gentiles? Yes, of the Gentiles also, since there is one God who will justify the circumcised by faith and the uncircumcised through faith. Do we then make void the law through faith? Certainly not! On the contrary, we establish the law." (Romans 3:27- 31 NKJV)

I am not telling you to go through your Bible to find the law to obey it. What I am saying is that we should run to Christ. Rely on Jesus! Rest all your cares and worries on Who and What He is; *Wonderful! Counselor! Prince of Peace! Mighty God!*

Concerning the Galatians, on more than one occasion, Paul rebuked the Galatians who tried to follow the law by works instead of by faith:

"O' foolish Galatians! Who has bewitched you that you should not obey the truth, before whose eyes Jesus Christ was clearly portrayed among you as crucified? This only I want to learn from you: Did you receive the Spirit by the works of the law, or by the hearing of faith? Are you so foolish? Having begun in the Spirit, are you now being made perfect by the flesh?" (Galatians 3:1- 3 NKJV)

Paul corrected the Galatians who thought that by observing the law that it would bring them perfection in Christ, and believed that their works would justify them.

"knowing that a man is not justified by the works of the law, but by the faith of Jesus Christ, even we have believed in Jesus Christ, that we might be justified by the faith of Christ, and not by the works of the law: for by the works of the law shall no flesh be justified. But if, while we seek to be justified by Christ, we ourselves also are found sinners, is, therefore, Christ, the minister of sin? God forbid. For if I build again the things which I destroyed, I make myself a transgressor." (Galatians 2:16-18 NKJV)

WALKING AFTER THE SPIRIT

What are you transgressing? The Bible says that we are transgressors of the law and Jesus said, *"I came not to do away with the law."* The rituals of the law are gone, but the judgment of the law still stands. The reason why the law was created, and the reason why it still exists today, is to deal with the unholy and the unrighteous. This is why when we look at the law we understand the absolute necessity in having Jesus in our lives; we can clearly see the reason that we need to run *to* Him and not run *from* Him.

In the above scripture *(Galatians 2:16-18)*, Paul said: *"For if I build again ..."* what are we rebuilding? In other words, if I am set free from homosexuality and I go back into it again does that make Jesus the justifier of homosexuality? Let me give you another example that relates to this question, if I am set free from anger, but I stay in anger, does that make Jesus the justifier of anger? To clarify our answer, Paul is saying that if we go back into the sin we were set free from, we become a transgressor of the law.

"But if, while we seek to be justified by Christ, we ourselves also are found sinners, is Christ therefore a minister of sin? Certainly not! For if I build again those things which I destroyed, I make myself a transgressor." Galatians 2:17-18 (NKJV)

Is there any communion at all between the law of the flesh and the law of the Spirit? No, there is none. The Bible says:

But I say, walk and live [habitually] in the [Holy]Spirit [responsive to and controlled and guided by the Spirit]; then you will certainly not gratify the cravings and desires of the flesh (of human nature without God). (Galatians 5:16 AMP)

But if you are guided (led) by the [Holy] Spirit, you are not subject to the Law. Galatians 5:18 AMP)

And those who belong to Christ Jesus (the Messiah) have crucified the flesh (the godless human nature) with its passions and appetites and desires. If we live by the [Holy] Spirit, let us also walk by the Spirit. [If by the Holy Spirit we have our life in God, let us go forward walking in line, our conduct controlled by the Spirit.]" (Galatians 5:24-25 AMPC)

You cannot serve God and mammon (Matthew 6:24).In other words, you cannot walk with God and walk with the devil. If an individual believes in serving God and man, read what the bible considers him to be

[For being as he is] a man of two minds (hesitating, dubious, irresolute), [he is] unstable and unreliable and uncertain about everything [he thinks, feels, decides]."(James 1:8 AMPC)

In addition, that person will receive nothing from the Lord. God tells us that when we die to the lust of the flesh, we put to death the affections of our lusts. If you follow your lusts, it will lead you away from God. That is why God tells us to die in these areas: *"Now the works of the flesh are evident, which are: adultery, fornication, uncleanness, licentiousness, idolatry, sorcery, hatred, contentions, jealousies, outbursts of wrath, selfish ambitions, dissensions, heresies, envy, murders, drunkenness, revelries, and the like; Of the which, I tell you beforehand, just as I also told you in time past, that those who practice such things will not inherit the kingdom of God."* (Galatians 5:19-21 NKJV)

Now Beloved, if God says they won't ... *"inherit the kingdom of God,"*is that the truth, or is that a lie? If it is the truth, then you need to ask God to put the reverence Fear of God in you. The lack of the fear of God in you is the first sign of rebellion, which is the same as witchcraft.

God is not mocked and whatever a man sows that shall he reap. This is one of the reasons that we must seek the Lord earnestly; so that we may reap what rightly belongs to us. I encourage you to sow the fruit of the Spirit, so you can reap all of Heaven's benefits: *"But the fruit of the Spirit is love, joy, peace, longsuffering, kindness, goodness, faithfulness, gentleness, self-control. Against such, there is no law."*(Galatians 5:22-23 NKJV)

Search the secrets of your heart and run to Christ in repentance.

Spiritual Nugget 9

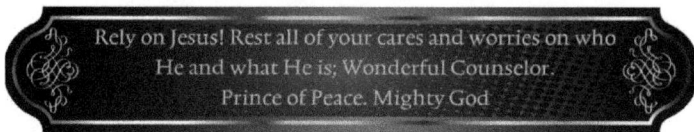

Rely on Jesus! Rest all of your cares and worries on who He and what He is; Wonderful Counselor. Prince of Peace. Mighty God

PART FOUR

CAPTURED AND PERFECTED

"But the fruit of the [Holy] Spirit [the work which His presence within accomplishes] is love, joy (gladness), peace, patience (an even temper, forbearance), kindness, goodness (benevolence), faithfulness, Gentleness (meekness, humility), self-control (self-restraint, continence). Against such things, there is no law [[a]that can bring a charge]."

Galatians 5:22-23 AMPC

CHAPTER TEN
THE GOLD NUGGET

There are many ways in which to examine your heart. I am going to introduce you to seven of these important ways. I am going to call them *Golden Nuggets,* and each one will allow you to become free. Once free, you will be able to fully follow Christ and walk in the fruit of the Spirit. We have learned from the previous chapters that when you walk in the Spirit of the living God, the law cannot touch us.

In order to help you understand each of the Golden Nuggets, I will ask you seven crucial questions to ponder and then I will provide the answers that will help guide you through the process of becoming and remaining free.

Golden Nugget Question Number 1:

How do you become free from walking in the law?

By walking in and living by the Spirit; in other words, by genuinely walking in God's Love. If you are not walking in God's Love, then the Spirit of the law will bring a curse of religion upon you. Although the law brings a curse, Jesus has set us free from that curse, but only if you remain in Him.

While remaining in Christ, and by walking in and living by His Spirit, our hearts are perfectly positioned for the process of transforming us into becoming more like Him. This transformation is the evidence of His indwelling within us. Jesus will never leave us broken, hurting, lacking, and in sin.

Real transformation comes from the inside and will produce Kingdom evidence on the outside.

This marks the difference between a genuine inward transformation which involves the spirit of God, or continuing to choose to operate out of fleshly desires. If we walk in the flesh then we practice the desires of the flesh; immorality, jealousy, anger, drunkenness, etc. However, if we make the decision to walk in the Spirit of God, then we are walking in His Living and Life Changing Word.

Golden Nugget Question Number 2:

Who is the Church of the Lord Jesus Christ?

The church of the Lord Jesus Christ is known as *Ekkliesia* the called-out ones. They are those who have crucified the flesh of their passions and their desires. Simply put, the true church is composed of those who are called by God. They are called not only outwardly, but inwardly by the Holy Spirit. When Jesus calls someone to discipleship, He is calling that person to Himself; to belong to Him, to follow Him, and to learn who He is and what He is all about.

Golden Nugget Question Number 3:

What are the passions and desires that those who belong to Christ have crucified?

The Bible is filled with answers to this question

But immorality (sexual vice) and all impurity] of lustful, rich, wasteful living] or greediness must not even be named among you, as is fitting and proper among saints (God's consecrated people). Let there be no filthiness (obscenity, indecency) nor foolish and sinful (silly and corrupt) talk, nor coarse jesting, which are not fitting or becoming; but instead voice your thankfulness [to God]. For be sure of this: that no person practicing sexual vice or impurity in thought or in life, or one who is covetous [who has lustful desire for the property of others and is greedy for gain]–for he [in effect] is an idolater–has any inheritance in the kingdom of Christ and of God." (Ephesians 5:3-5 AMPC)

as well as *"Do you not know that the unrighteous and the wrongdoers will not inherit or have any share in the kingdom of God? Do not be deceived (misled): neither the impure and immoral, nor idolaters, nor adulterers, nor those who participate in homosexuality"* (1 Corinthians 6:9 AMPC)

There is also the scripture: *"For you are still carnal. For where there are envy, strife, and divisions, among you are you not carnal and behaving like mere men?"* (1 Corinthians 3:3 NKJV)

Golden Nugget Question Number 4:

What are envy and strife and why are people dealing with them?

Scripture tells us that *"A heart at peace gives life to the body, but envy rots the bones"(Prov. 14:30 NKJV)*. Envy is defined as *a feeling of discontent and resentment aroused by another's desirable possessions or qualities, accompanied by a strong desire to have them for oneself.* It is an emotion that we each feel from time to time. However, if it is allowed to become dominant in our lives, it will warp our perspectives. Envy will keep us from realizing our personal potential and, in cases like this, will lead us into destructive behavior. Without question, envy impedes our growth towards spiritual maturity.

Strife is defined as *bitter discord, conflict, or antagonism towards others.* It is often represented as hidden, repressed anger and can bring about judgment, gossiping, backbiting, as well as thinking too highly of oneself. Strife is often exhibited by arguing, bickering, heated disagreements, and angry undercurrents.

Strife keeps us bound in many ways. Both envy and strife lock us in a battle which keeps us distracted and focused on the dark and destructive things of this world. They act similarly to a handcuff or ball and chain, and their purpose is to paralyze and inhibit us. They each restrict our thoughts of love and peace and place them instead on thoughts of negativity, bitterness, fear, and anger.

Golden Nugget Question Number 5:

Are you being honest with yourself?

The truth is that everyone struggles with something. You may have heard someone says something similar such as; "*Well praise God, I do not have to deal with anything. I am perfect. There isn't anything wrong in my life. I never struggle. I am a minister of the Lord Jesus Christ.*"

What a lie! Let us be real and above all honest.

We should not walk around wearing a false mask in order to fool the outside world as well as ourselves. Nor, should we pretend that everything is ideal within us spiritually. This is not a game; the eternal destiny of our soul is at stake. We are commanded to be perfect as our Father in Heaven is perfect. In some Bible translations, the word perfect means "mature" (spiritually).

Paul said it to the Philippians in this manner

"I press on toward the goal to win the [supreme and heavenly] prize to which God in Christ Jesus is calling us upward. So let those [of us] who are spiritually mature and full-grown have this mind and hold these convictions; and if in any respect you have a different attitude of mind, God will make that clear to you also. Only let us hold true to what we have already attained and walk and order our lives by that. Brethren together follow my example and observe those who live after the pattern we have set for you." (Philippians 3:14-17 AMPC).

In other words, we should be holy as Jesus Christ is holy. We should purify ourselves just as He is pure.

"And everyone who has this hope [resting] on Him cleanses (purifies) himself just as He is pure (chaste, undefiled, guiltless)." (1 John 3:3 AMPC)

And we should walk as we see He walked.

Whoever says he abides in Him ought [as a personal debt] to walk and conduct himself in the same way in which He walked and conducted Himself. (John 2:6 (AMPC)

What did Paul say in the scripture above? Imitate me as imitate Christ.

Golden Nugget Question Number 6:

What is the spiritual impact of jealousy?

Jealousy is the resentment felt against a rival, or against a person who is enjoying more success or a greater advantage than we are.

"Anger is cruel and fury overwhelming, but who can stand before jealousy?" (Proverb 27:4 NIV)

This Scripture implies that jealousy is often a hidden corrosion which corrupts our motives, thoughts, and actions. Remember the devastating results of King Saul's jealousy towards David and how it twisted and warped his life? Jealousy can do harm in many ways; left unchecked it can destroy friendships and family bonds. Often born out of fear, jealousy makes matters worse. In addition, by allowing it to gain a foothold, its effects bring only insecurity, pain, and destruction.

"Jealous" is defined as "*very watchful or careful in guarding or keeping*", and "*resentfully envious*". Envy is defined as "*a feeling of discontent*" and "*ill will because of another's advantages, possessions, etc.; resentful dislike of another who has something that one desires.*" Jealousy has stronger emotions attached.

Golden Nugget Question Number 7

Who are we to imitate?

The Bible makes this very clear; we are to be imitators of God. *Ephesians 5:1* says to be followers [imitators] of God like little children. Another translation says,

"Therefore be imitators of God [copy Him and follow His example, as well-beloved children imitate their father]." (Ephesians 5:1 AMP)

Therefore, we are not to walk, talk, and act like the world, but we are to walk, talk, and act like God. The Bible says, *"Therefore since these [great] promises are ours, beloved, let us cleanse ourselves from everything that contaminates and defiles body and spirit, and bring [our] consecration to completeness in the [reverential] fear of God."* (II Corinthians 7:1 AMPC)

With the *Golden Nugget* questions that we have studied and answered here, I pray that you have examined your heart and have allowed God's Word to change you as you imitate Christ. When you come to the saving grace of the knowledge and revelation of the Lord Jesus Christ, you should immediately begin to cleanse yourself from the filthiness of the flesh.

"For the law made nothing perfect; on the other hand, there is bringing in of a better hope, through which we draw near to God." (Hebrews 7:19 NKJV)

GOLDEN NUGGETS FOR THE SOUL

In order that we may see even more evidence of His tangible Love, the Holy Spirit is always ready and willing to reveal Christ to us in every way. Jesus' Thoughts and His Actions are always declaring His Heart towards us. Moreover, His compassion towards you and I confirm within our spirit that the absolute and proper truth resides in His words.

Jesus can speak to us right where we are, no matter what our circumstances. When He speaks to us, we can experience various emotions; we may cry, become joyful, and we may even experience anger. Whatever the emotions that we may experience, the most important thing that we should do is to allow change, through Christ, to happen.

I trust that you believe, and agree, with me that Jesus is an amazing Savior. He is a Savior who proves to us that if we give Him our shortcomings, we can become more like Him in every area of our lives.

If you desire a true *Golden Nugget* to forever reside in your soul, give Christ the opportunity to mold you into someone who is pliable; someone with whom He can work. If you do not, you will only find yourself fighting God, and the Lord does not desire that for you or for me. He has an excellent and unique plan for your life, please allow Him to fulfill it according to the abounding love that He has for you.

"For I know the plans and thoughts that I have for you,' says the LORD, 'plans for peace and well-being and not for disaster, to give you a future and a hope. Then you will call on Me, and you will come and pray to Me, and I will hear [your voice], and I will listen to you. Then [with a deep longing] you will seek Me and require Me [as a vital necessity] and [you will] find Me when you search for Me with all your heart."
(Jeremiah 29:11-13 AMP)

Christ Jesus has many ways in which to allow our souls to become renewed by His transforming Word. These life, heart, and soul transformations come only by doing and living out His Word both in and through our lives. There are many blessings and treasures that are given to the children of God, and one of these treasures is that no one is ever beyond His reach.

Check the Blueprint (God's Holy Bible) and trust me, Jesus' Hands are all over it. Found within the Bible's pages, even the most lost person can be

EXPOSING THE SECRETS OF THE HEART

embraced with all of the compassion, love, and hope that they will ever need. What an awesome Savior we serve!

"Whenever, though, they turn to face God as Moses did, God removes the veil, and there they are–face-to- face! They suddenly recognize that God is a living, personal presence, not a piece of chiseled stone. And when God is personally present, a living Spirit, that old, constricting legislation is recognized as obsolete.

We're free of it! All of us! Nothing between us and God, our faces shining with the brightness of his face. And so, we are transfigured much like the Messiah, our lives gradually becoming brighter and more beautiful as God enters our lives and we become like him." (2 Corinthians 3:16-18 MSG)

Spiritual Nugget: 10

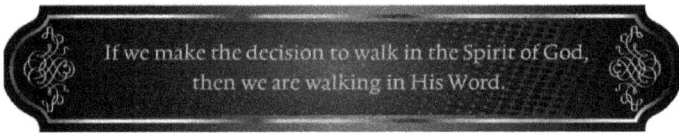

If we make the decision to walk in the Spirit of God, then we are walking in His Word.

"But let endurance and steadfastness and patience have full play and do a thorough work, so that you may be [people] perfectly and fully developed [with no defects], lacking in nothing.

James 1:4 AMPC

CHAPTER ELEVEN
BE PERFECT

By walking in the fruit of the Spirit, you will mature in the things of God; being made perfect, complete, and lacking nothing.

We have learned from previous chapters that Christ in us is the hope of glory (Colossians 1:27). When you came to the knowledge of the Lord Jesus Christ, God gave you the ability to put sin to death

"Therefore, since Christ suffered in the flesh [and died for us], arm yourselves [like warriors] with the same purpose [being willing to suffer for doing what is right and pleasing God], because whoever has suffered in the flesh [being like-minded with Christ] is done with [intentional] sin [having stopped pleasing the world], so that he can no longer spend the rest of his natural life living for human appetites and desires, but [lives] for the will and purpose of God." (1 Peter 4: 1-2 AMP)

Romans 6:1-23 (AMPC) states:

"What shall we say [to all this]? Are we to remain in sin in order that God's grace (favor and mercy) may multiply and overflow? Certainly not! How can we who died to sin live in it any longer? Are you ignorant of the fact that all of us who have been baptized into Christ Jesus were baptized into His death? We were buried therefore with Him by the baptism into death, so that just as Christ was raised from the dead by the glorious [power] of the Father, so we too might [habitually] live and behave in newness of life.

For if we have become one with Him by sharing a death like His, we shall also be [one with Him in sharing] His resurrection [by a new life lived for God]. We know that our old (unrenewed) self was nailed to the cross with Him in order that [our] body [which is the instrument] of sin might be made ineffective and inactive for evil, that we might no longer be the slaves of sin. For when a man dies, he is freed (loosed, delivered) from [the power of] sin [among men].

Now if we have died with Christ, we believe that we shall also live with Him, Because we know that Christ (the Anointed One), being once raised from the dead, will never die again; death no longer has power over Him. For by the death He died, He died to sin [ending His relation to it] once for all; and the life that He lives, He is living to God [in unbroken fellowship with Him. Even so consider yourselves also dead to sin and your relation to it broken, but alive to God [living in unbroken fellowship with Him] in Christ Jesus.

Let not sin therefore rule as king in your mortal (short-lived, perishable) bodies, to make you yield to its cravings and be subject to its lusts and evil passions. Do not continue offering or yielding your bodily members [and faculties] to sin as instruments (tools) of wickedness. But offer and yield yourselves to God as though you have been raised from the dead to [perpetual] life, and your bodily members [and faculties] to God, presenting them as implements of righteousness.

For sin shall not [any longer] exert dominion over you, since now you are not under Law [as slaves], but under grace [as subjects of God's favor and mercy. What then [are we to conclude]? Shall we sin because we live not under Law but under God's favor and mercy? Certainly not! Do you not know that if you continually surrender yourselves to anyone to do his will, you are the slaves of him whom you obey, whether that be to sin, which leads to death, or to obedience which leads to righteousness (right doing and right standing with God)?

But thank God, though you were once slaves of sin, you have become obedient with all your heart to the standard of teaching in which you were instructed and to which you were committed. And having been set free from sin, you have become the servants of righteousness (of conformity to the divine will in thought, purpose, and action).

I am speaking in familiar human terms because of your natural limitations. For as you yielded your bodily members [and faculties] as servants to impurity and everincreasing lawlessness, so now yield your bodily members [and faculties] once for all as servants to righteousness (right being and doing) [which leads] to sanctification. For when you were slaves of sin, you were free in regard to righteousness. But then what benefit (return) did you get from the things of which you are now ashamed?

[None] for the end of those things is death. But now since you have been set free from sin and have become the slaves of God, you have your present reward in holiness, and its end is eternal life. For the wages which sin pays is death, but the [bountiful] free gift of God is eternal life through (in union with) Jesus Christ our Lord.

I do not mean to indicate that you will not have to deal with your thought life after you quit the physical act, however, all of it must be surrendered to the Lord. It is a process, and it is perfected when you yield to the work of the Holy Spirit.

The Spirit of God helps you to put sin to death. As we allow the fear of God to help perfect holiness within us, we become more like Him. God says that you *can* be perfect. The word "perfect" simply means to be "mature" and in "wholeness." Paul prayed that the God of peace would make us perfect. The Word says

"Now may the God of peace [Who is the Author and the Giver of peace], Who brought again from among the dead our Lord Jesus, that great Shepherd of the sheep, by the blood [that sealed, ratified] the everlasting agreement (covenant, testament), Strengthen (complete, perfect) and make you what you ought to be and equip you with everything good that you may carry out His will; [while He Himself] works in you and accomplishes that which is pleasing in His sight, through Jesus Christ (the Messiah); to Whom be the glory forever and ever (to the ages of the ages). Amen (so be it)." (Hebrews 13:20-21 APMC)

THE PERFECT WALK

I have heard many people teach, "You can't be perfect," and I personally do not believe that since it is contrary to the Bible. Jesus Christ can change you totally to become just like Him.

The Bible states, "For those whom He foreknew [of whom He was aware and loved beforehand], He also destined from the beginning [foreordaining them] to be molded into the image of His Son [and share inwardly His likeness], that He might become the firstborn among many brethren. And those whom He thus foreordained, He also called; and those whom He called, He also justified (acquitted, made righteous, putting them into right standing with Himself). And those whom He justified, He also glorified [raising them to a heavenly dignity and condition or state of being]." (Romans 8:29-30 AMPC)

If you do not believe this, you are walking in doubt and unbelief. There are many people who do not receive their healing simply because they do not believe the Bible. They say, *"Well, that was for back then."* They also believe this about speaking in tongues and many of the other Biblical promises that God has freely given to us in order to bless His church.

The Scripture says,

"We are glad when we are weak [since God's power comes freely through us], but you [by comparison] are strong. We also pray for this, that you be made complete [fully restored, growing and maturing in godly character and spirit-pleasing your heavenly Father by the life you live]." (2 Corinthians 13:9 AMP)

Remember what Paul said to the Corinthians: *"I want you to be everything God wants you to be. I want you to be complete."* The word *entire* in the Greek language is *holoklero* meaning "complete, sound in every part." This word is synonymous with the Greek word *teleioteros* (or "perfect,") and remember the word perfection simply means to be "mature" and in "wholeness", thus indicating the development of every grace into maturity.

Take a look at what the book of James says about trials and patience: *"My brethren, count it all joy when you fall into various trials."* (James 1:2 NKJV)

Falling into various trials does not sound like fun, does it? Do you know why we do not like it when the fire comes? Because no one has ever thoroughly explained to us about the gold that we become by going through the fire.

Some people may think, *"I am getting beat up by the devil."* Do you know why God allows that to happen to you? He allows it to happen in order to test your heart. He wants to find out who you love more; Him or the devil. As you go through the trial and that fire, God will perfect you into a vessel of gold.

I have learned to take on trials and count it all joy because I know that in the fire I will become more like Jesus. Was not there a fourth man in the fire with Shadrach, Meshach, and Abed-nego? Who do you think the fourth man was? It was Jesus. They had to count it all joy as they walked through the fire with patience.

The scripture says, *"And let endurance have its perfect result and do a thorough work, so that you may be perfect and completely developed [in your faith], lacking in nothing."* (James 1:4 AMP)

There is that word *perfect* again. The word *entire* in the Greek language is *holokleros,* meaning "complete, sound in every part." This word is synonymous with the Greek word teleioteros or *perfect,* which teaches us to walk in the mature status of character as we continue to develop.

Take another look at this scripture from another translation

"But let patience have its perfect work so that you may be mature and complete, not lacking anything." (James 1:4 KJV)

You can be complete. Now let's take a moment and look at this from a different standpoint, does anger, unforgiveness, fornication, bitterness, lesbianism, lying, cheating, or cursing come from God?

The Bible gives us a clear answer:

"Therefore, since these [great] promises are ours, beloved, let us cleanse ourselves from everything that contaminates and defiles body and spirit, and bring [our] consecration to completeness in the [reverential] fear of God." (II Corinthians 7:1 AMPC)

Therefore, the things of the flesh are not of God. So, what is of God?

"But the fruit of the Spirit is love, joy, peace, longsuffering, kindness, goodness, faithfulness, Gentleness, self-control. Against such, there is no law." (Galatians 5:22-23 NKJV).

Did you notice what the Word said, that the law could not touch the fruit of the Spirit of God; it is the place of immunity protection or exemption from something, especially an obligation or penalty and safety.

Guarding your heart with the fruit of the Spirit empowers you to be mature, complete, and lacking nothing in the things of God. When the Lord takes hold of you (if you allow Him to), and you are made whole, there is not much that will be missing from your life. God does not make it a habit of coming against your own will. Although, keep in mind that the Lord can be very influential at times.

The Holy Spirit can create change in us in ways that will cause us to become better in Christ and a love haven to His people. God will empower us with comfort (and the ability to love the unlovable), so that we may remain in the characterization of completeness and maturity, which is the Spirit of Christ.

I believe that the Holy Spirit can do certain things even if we do not desire to change. Trust me; it can become much easier to love others (even those who hurt us) as we learn to yield to the Holy Spirit.

Spiritual Nugget 11

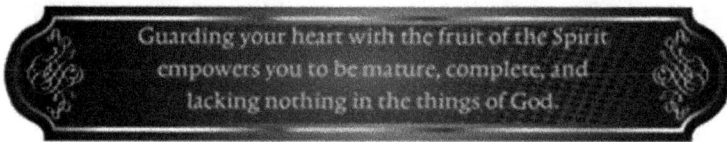

Guarding your heart with the fruit of the Spirit empowers you to be mature, complete, and lacking nothing in the things of God.

"You shall have no other gods before Me."

Exodus 20:3 NKJV

CHAPTER TWELVE
YOUR SECRETS

Allow me the privilege of asking you another question. Do you really want to know how to walk in the Fruit of Gods Spirit with the evidence of it in your life? Then take a few minutes to ponder these questions.

What are the secrets that you **are** *afraid to let go because you believe it will cost you everything?*

Before I gave my life to Jesus Christ, my hidden secret was adultery. I knew back then that if I told my wife what I had done, she would have left me. After I gave my life to him, I knew that God was going to restore everything to me. However, I also knew that he was going to test me to see if I loved him more than the sin I had kept hidden. I had learned from reading the word that if I loved anything more than I loved God that it was idolatry.

For example, if I love my ministry, my family, or my children more than I love God that is considered idolatry. God said it best when He spoke. *"Thou shalt have no other gods before me."* (Exodus 20:3-5 NKJV)
What He is saying here is *I am your source for everything I am a jealous God, and nothing else shall take my place.*

Do you want to see the glory of God? If the answer is yes, then you must get real with the Lord. God was in the Holy of Holies because it was clean and without sin. Therefore, Jesus will cleanse every temple once He comes in.

Do you not discern and understand that you [the whole church at Corinth] are God's temple (His sanctuary), and that God's Spirit has His permanent dwelling in you [to be at home in you, collectively as a church and also individually]? (1 Corinthians 3:16 AMPC)

During biblical times, they did not have what you and I have been given to us by Jesus; His Blood and His Spirit. Today, we are washed by the Blood of Jesus, and it is only His Blood and His Spirit which can purify and justify us.

One night many years ago in a church service, my brother Craig McNally and I stood up and said, "*Here is a line. We are on the side where the Holy of Holies is, and we are in here with Jesus. How right are you with God? Can you walk across to where we are in the Holy of Holies?*"

The fear of God hit me, and I stepped away from the Holy of Holies and went to the other side. At that point, I got a reality check. I immediately made some things right with the Lord in my heart before I could step back to the other side in the holy of Holies.

Due to making unrighteous choices, many Christians are dying in their sin every day along with those in the world without Christ. Listen to what God says about His Wrath and Ungodliness.

"For God's [holy] wrath and indignation are revealed from heaven against all ungodliness and unrighteousness of men, who in their wickedness repress and hinder the truth and make it inoperative..." (Romans 1:18 AMPC).

It Is God's plan for you and I to make the right choices; His Love and the provision which He has prepared for us. However, rather than accepting His Love, many people prefer to walk in disobedience which results in their receiving God's wrath instead. This is not God's plan for their lives, especially since He came to saved us from His wrath.

"For God did not appoint us to wrath, but to obtain salvation through our Lord Jesus Christ ..." (1 Thessalonians 5:9 NKJV).

Despite this truth, we would rather agree with the devil than agree with God. As a result of this unfortunate and life-altering choice, the wrath of God comes upon the sons of disobedience. Nonetheless, the Holy Spirit wants to expose the secrets and deceptions within your heart in order to bring true freedom from what is holding us captive, and to deliver us from what is keeping us bound.

Here is the question which you must sincerely ask yourself.

What is the secret in your life that is keeping you from the presence of God?

You must examine your heart thoroughly for hidden things pertaining to sin. When you do, Jesus will show you what is truly in your heart, how much He deeply Loves you, and how much you need Him.

Taking this necessary step of examining your heart will bring you to a place of real intimacy with Him. It is when you become closer to God {through His love and His affection} that He will share His Heart for you.

This incredible heart-searching experience will teach you something about God which shall never be taken away from you; the truth about the Heart of the Lord. What is the truth of the Heart of the Lord? **LIBERTY**! For within Him is marvelous liberty.

Within God's Presence bondages are broken, lives are transformed, deliverances take place, and in His Presence is the fullness of joy. For this reason, because of who He truly is, the Lord gets all of the glory!

Let's read what Colossians has to say on the matter: *"See to it that no one carries you off as spoil or makes you yourselves captive by his so-called philosophy and intellectualism and vain deceit (idle fancies and plain nonsense), following human tradition (men's ideas of the material rather than the spiritual world), just crude notions following the rudimentary and elemental. Teachings of the universe and disregarding [the teachings of] Christ (the Messiah).*

For in Him the whole fullness of Deity (the Godhead) continues to dwell in bodily form [giving complete expression of the divine nature]. And you are in Him, made full and having come to the fullness of life [in Christ you too are filled with the Godhead–Father, Son, and Holy Spirit– and reach full spiritual stature]. And He is the Head of all rule and authority [of every angelic principality and power]." (Colossians 2:8-10 AMPC)

I hear people quote the verse, *"Therefore submit to God. Resist the devil and he will flee from you."* (James 4:7 NKJV).

You submit to God by obeying him. *And having been made perfect [uniquely equipped and prepared as Savior and retaining His integrity amid opposition], He became the source of eternal salvation [an eternal inheritance] to all those who obey Him."* (Hebrews 5:9 AMP)

How do you resist the devil? By submitting to God. *"For there are three that bear witness in heaven: The Father, the Word, and the Holy Spirit; and these three are one. And there are three that bear witness on earth: The Spirit, the water, and the blood; and these three agree as one."* (1 John 5:7, 8 NKJV)

There are three in Heaven that agree: The Father, the Word (Jesus), and the Holy Spirit. They are all in total communion. There are three on Earth that agree as well: The world, the flesh, and the devil

"For all that is in the world–the lust of the flesh, the lust of the eyes, and the pride of life–is not of the Father but is of the world. (1 John 2:16 NKJV)

You have God and His Two and the devil and his two. Someone is a counterfeit, and it is not God. It is the devil. He accomplishes his goals by using the same strategy as the Lord's. All sinful nature agrees with satan, and your born-again spirit-man agree with Father God.

Has your nature ever changed?

We are each made in the likeness and image of Almighty God, right? The Word of God says: *"Let Us (Father, Son, Holy Spirit) make man in Our image, according to Our likeness [not physical, but a spiritual personality and moral likeness]; and let them have complete authority over the fish of the sea, the birds of the air, the cattle, and over the entire earth, and over everything that creeps and crawls on the earth."* (Genesis 1:26 AMP)

I would like for you to commit to memory the fact that when Adam sinned and fell, our nature did change: *"And Adam lived one hundred and thirty years, and begot a son in **his own likeness**, after his image; and called his name Seth."* (Genesis 5:3 NKJV, emphasis added.)

My point is this, in whose image did he beget a son? The answer is *in his own image.* That is a little different from the likeness and image of God, correct? Therefore, according to the Word of God, it changes. When Adam fell, we took on the sinful nature.

God wants to expose the secrets of men's hearts. He wants you to know that there is real power in the name of Jesus Christ. When we choose not to believe that the Lord Jesus will do what He says He will do (both in and through your life) we are in unbelief. Consider the Israelites; the

Bible says because of unbelief, they could not enter into His rest."
(Hebrews 3:11 NKJV)

Now, here is a power question

Do you know why we do not believe God's Word?

In simple terms, we do not believe His Word because we do not put the Word into action in our lives. We forget that for every action there is a reaction. A struggling Christian may say, *"God, I know you can make me into an Image Bearer, nevertheless, if you need me to do the transformation and bear your image and likeness as taught in Genesis chapter one, there is no way I can manifest this on my own."*

As an apostle of Jesus Christ, I say to you that you are more than able to become all that God has called you to be. In the Bible, it says,

"And my God shall supply all your need according to His riches in glory by Christ Jesus." (Philippians 4:19 NKVJ)

That promise from His Word is all you need. Everything that you will ever have need, God will supply it, according to his will.

Again, the Bible tells us, *"For the Lord God is a Sun and Shield; the Lord bestows [present] Grace and favor and [future] glory (honor, splendor, and heavenly bliss)! No good thing will He withhold from those who walk uprightly."* (Psalms 84:11 AMPC)

God wants to take care of you, but you must want that too. Jesus paid a great price in dying for you so that you might live for Him, but the decision is yours.

I preached a message once titled *"You Can Get Another Jesus."* What was so eye-opening about this message was that, as the Bible illustrates in Galatians the second letter to the Corinthian people, you can get another Jesus, another spirit, and another gospel: *"But even if we, or an angel from heaven, preach any other gospel to you than what we have preached to you, let him be accursed."* (Galatians 1:8 NKJV)

For [you seem willing to allow it] if one comes and preaches another Jesus whom we have not preached, or if you receive a different spirit from the

one you received or a different gospel from the one you accepted. You tolerate all this beautifully [welcoming the deception]. (2 Corinthians 11:4 AMP)

This scripture teaches us about another *form* of Jesus. This is a form of Jesus that most people accept and put up with; a Jesus and a gospel which has no *power*. This form of Jesus is a powerless misrepresentation of the real Christ Jesus. This *other* Jesus and gospel cannot forgive you of your sin, it cannot save you, and it cannot heal you. This form of Jesus does not even have the power to get you out of debt.

Yet, the True Jesus who is in the Holy Bible can do so much for you and I; wondrous, life-giving, hope-filled blessings and eternal gains are what He brings. However, He does it the way that He wants to do it. It is not, *"God, come down here and help me out."* God wants to do it His way because His way is absolutely infallible. When we do it His way, He will change our lives for the better.

I know this to be true because He truly changed my life and my family's life. When I was in the world, I enjoyed smoking, drinking, partying, and swearing. I did it because I liked it. I also committed adultery because it felt good to my flesh. The inward man in me did not like it, but the flesh loved it. This is why we do wrong things - because it agrees with the flesh.

Consequently, I now realize that the things that I used to do, and the beliefs that I use to hold have no meaning.

Here is a simple question for you - *Why do you get up in the morning and eat breakfast?* You eat breakfast because it feels good to your flesh and it is what everybody does when they get up in the morning. Here is another question that may be considered to be more difficult *"Why are there so many Christians who struggle with smoking?"* Why do they do it? Plainly, because it feels good to the flesh. I know because I smoked for twenty years.

"and you shall know the truth, and the truth shall make you free." (John 8:32 AKJV)

Take a look at this verse: *"For to be carnally minded is death, but to be spiritually minded is life and peace. Because the carnal mind is enmity against God: for it is not subject to the law of God, nor indeed can be. So then, those who are in the flesh cannot please God."* (Romans 8:6-8 AMP)

From this scripture, we learn that those who live and operate in the flesh cannot please God.

The Word of God goes on to say, *"for all have sinned and fall short of the glory of God."* (Romans 3:23 NKJV)

The truth is that we all need to get real with ourselves and one another. We must admit that we need help and that we do not have all of the answers. In effect, getting real may help us to become free from the traps of submitting to the flesh.

When we get real with God, God gets real with us. This happens so that when you wholeheartedly deal with your sin, it allows you to become completely free. When you begin to honestly admit that you need God's help He *will* indeed show up for you. I have seen Him do it countless times everywhere that I go.

There are times when some people say, *"I'm getting my brains beat out by the devil,"* instead of saying, *"He's under my feet!"* Yet, there are areas in our lives where he is not under our feet, he is on top of us beating us down.

God said, "...Let My people go so they can worship Me." (Exodus 5:1 NKJV)

Instinctively, your spirit wants to worship God because He is who you were created after. God said, *"But the hour is coming, and now is, when the true worshipers will worship the Father in spirit and truth; for the Father is seeking such to worship Him. God is Spirit, and those who worship Him must worship in spirit and truth."* (John 4:23-24 NKJV)

Let us look at this scripture: "But if you are led by the Spirit, you are not under the law." (Galatians 5:18 NKJV)

This is the key – His Spirit must lead you! However, your flesh and the devil do not desire that you should worship God in spirit and in truth, yet The Messiah says,

"...I tell you that if these should keep silent, the stones would immediately cry out." (Luke 19:40 NKJV)

We are so busy looking at one another and saying, *"At least I am not as bad as they are, and I'm not doing what they are doing."* That is self-righteousness.

The mind of Christ is in your heart and that which you received at salvation. You either have the mind of Christ, or you have the mind of satan. If you do not have the mind of Christ, then you have the mind of satan; this is the mark on the forehead. God led the children of Israel with a strong right hand and if you are not being led by God's right Hand, then it means that you are doing it by your own right hand.

In the book of Revelation, it says that you will receive the mark of the beast either on your forehead or on your right hand. Do you know what you are saying if you receive the mark of the beast? The Bible says that once you receive the mark on your right hand or forehead, you have forever denied God and there is no turning back. God forbid!

"And he deceives those who dwell on the earth by those signs which he was granted to do in the sight of the beast, telling those who dwell on the earth to make an image to the beast who was wounded by the sword and lived. He was granted power to give breath to the image of the beast, that the image of the beast should both speak and cause as many as would not worship the image of the beast to be killed.

He causes all, both small and great, rich and poor, free and slave, to receive a mark on their right hand or on their foreheads, and that no one may buy or sell except one who *Has the mark or the name of the beast, or the number of his name. Here is wisdom. Let him who has understanding calculate the number of the beast, for it, is the number of a man: His number is 666."*
(Revelation 13:14 – 18 NKJV)

This Revelation has been revealed for those who will be left behind so that we may be mindful and aware that there are consequences to the choices that we make.

FIGHT THE FLESH TO FREEDOM

Who is the Church of the Lord Jesus Christ? The Church are those who have crucified their flesh along with their passions and desires.

What keeps you from the Presence of God? Sin does.

Sin is you simply saying, *"It's all about me - It's my way."* A prime example is satan in Isaiah 14:12-17

"How art thou fallen from heaven, O Lucifer, son of the morning! How art thou cut down to the ground, which didst weaken the nations! For thou hast said in thine heart, I will ascend into heaven; I will exalt my throne above the stars of God: I will sit also upon the mount of the congregation, in the sides of the north: I will ascend above the heights of the clouds; I will be like the most High. Yet thou shalt be brought down to hell, to the sides of the pit. They that see thee shall narrowly look upon thee, and consider thee, saying, is this the man that made the earth to tremble, that did shake kingdoms; That made the world as a wilderness, and destroyed the cities thereof; that opened not the house of his prisoners?"

God does not say that we should do things our way, God says that we should do things His way. If you do things His way, He says, *I will lead you to the Promised Land.* There were about three million people that left Egypt, but only a handful of them made it to the Promised Land. Why? Disobedience.

Therefore, do not let the devil lie to you; there is only one way to heaven and that is by living by the example Jesus has already set for us. God is coming back for a blameless and spotless Bride. "that he might present it to himself a glorious church, not having spot, or wrinkle, or any such thing, but that it should be holy and without blemish." (Ephesians 5:27 NKJV)

The Bible states *"Pursue peace with all people, and holiness, without which no one will see the Lord:"*(Hebrews 12:14 NKJV)

"And let him turn away from evil, and do good; Let him seek peace and pursue it. For the eyes of the Lord are on the righteous, And His ears unto their supplication: But the face of the Lord is against them that do evil." (1 Peter 3:11 ASV)

God will never ask what denomination you are because He does not care about traditions and denominations. He only asks that you obey Him.

Week after week, I see people approach the altar ensnared in the bondage of sin. They are covered in sin and do not want to deal with ***SELF.***

They do not want to admit to, or give up, the sin which they are involved in. Furthermore, they do not want to humble themselves under the mighty hand of God.

As for me, I do not want to miss God. I do not care if I miss everything else because, to me, it is all rubbish. I do not want to spend an eternity in hell. I do not want to miss Christ. More than anything, I want to go home to be with Him. I want to do what Jesus wants me to do. Unfortunately, some people will not make it. The Bible reads,

"And then I will declare to them, "I never knew you; depart from Me, you who practice lawlessness!" (Matthew 7:23 NKJV)

I do not want to stand before Jesus and hear Him say that I held anything back from Him. Yet, there are a lot of things many people hold back from God. They do this because they know that if they truly allow Him to work within their hearts and lives that it may lead to consequences. When I committed adultery, there were consequences that I had to deal with. It is not an easy road to deal with the results of our sins, but God is there. I made mistakes, but God met me at every avenue

I know a man that embezzled fifty thousand dollars because of the Y2K scare. The devil lied to him and told him that everything in the world was ending. The enemy told him that his embezzlement was ok, that he was not doing anything wrong. However, what he did not understand was that if the world had indeed ended, he would have been doomed to hell.

The end of the world did not occur, and the man repented of his sin. God reached out of Heaven with never ending mercy and forgave him. After his repentance, the he called everyone from whom he had taken money and each one forgave him of his sin, and his debt. Only God can do that.

In other words, if the Lord did it for him, He will definitely do it for you and I. He will most assuredly make our lives right again, if we let him.

"Come close to God, and He will come close to you. [Recognize that you are] sinners, get your soiled hands clean; [realize that you have been disloyal] wavering individuals with divided interests, and purify your hearts [of your spiritual adultery]." (James 4:8 AMPC)

God did not say that we would not go through fires He said that He would go through the fire with us. The Body of Christ is often battling with sin within their lives, but many do not like to confront it head on.

How do you handle sin? You handle it by repenting {turning from the sin} and submitting yourself to God.

When satan tries to bring temptations back into your life, continuing to resist him will cause him to flee. Resist the flesh, the desires, and the temptations of sin and draw closer to God each time

So be subject to God. Resist the devil [stand firm against him], and he will flee from you. Come close to God and He will come close to you. [Recognize that you are] sinners, get your soiled hands clean; [realize that you have been disloyal] wavering individuals with divided interests, and purify your hearts [of your spiritual adultery]." (James 4:7-8 AMPC)

In other words, draw near to God with all your heart and the devil has to go!

I used to struggle with lust. My wife will tell you this as well. I would have to run out of stores because of the women that were in there. They were not doing anything wrong, it was a spirit of lust that was drawing me.

I said, *"No God, I love you more than I love myself."* Then I said to my wife, *"Janet, pray for me; the devil tried once again to put lust on me."*

I made a covenant with my eyes for God. I asked *"God, make my eyes pure." Today,* I no longer deal with lust, and it is only through God that I will never again.

The Bible states, *For all that is in the world - the lust of the flesh, the lust of the eyes and the pride of life - is not of the Father but is of the world."* (I John 2:16 NKJV)

Please allow me to remind you again that when you draw near to God, He will draw near to you. As you press into God, He will press into you, but we must put forth a determined effort to do so. Often, we go through the motions of religious rituals, but when God says that there will be a cost to us then we draw back and give up. Yet, we know deep within ourselves that we cannot afford to draw back, that we must continue to press into God.

What is that cost? It is simply giving up the things you like to do that are contrary to His Word.

You can overcome anything by drawing near to God and resisting lustful temptations when they come your way.

"...but each man is tempted, when he is drawn away of his own lust, and enticed." (James 1:14 ASV)

The Father would not tell you to put to death the deeds of the flesh if it were not possible. It *is* possible! There are times when I say to people *"Come on, let's go all the way to the throne of God together,"* and they just look at me strangely. It is as if they say, *"This is as far as I want to go. I am comfortable right where I am."* To me, that is idolatry because they will not give up what they secretly love in their hearts more than they love God Himself.

Take every thought captive and be ready to put away anything that will exalt itself against the knowledge of God to the obedience of Jesus Christ. You can do it!

"For the weapons of our warfare are not carnal, but mighty through God to the pulling down of strongholds; Casting down imaginations, and every high thing that exalteth itself against the knowledge of God and bringing into captivity every thought to the obedience of Christ; And having in a readiness to revenge all disobedience, when your obedience is fulfilled." (2 Corinthians 10: 4 - 6 KJV)

In conclusion, let me leave with you one of my favorite scriptures: *"I can do all things through Christ who strengthens me."* (Philippians 4:13 NKJV)

My God is big enough! He is the King of Kings and the Lord of Lords! His Name is Jesus of Nazareth! He has transformed me into a new creation. He wants to take each of us deeper into the Holy of Holies. Do you want to go in? All you have to do is expose the hidden secrets of your heart, so you may be FREE!

So I end this verse in Deuteronomy 30: 19-20

"I call heaven and earth as witnesses today against you, that I have set before you life and death, blessing and cursing: therefore choose life, that both you and your descendants may live; that you may love the LORD your God, that you may obey His voice, and that you may cling to Him, for He is your life and the length of your days; and that you may dwell in

the land which the LORD swore to your fathers, to Abraham, Isaac, and Jacob, to give them."

Spiritual Nugget 12

Take every thought captive and be ready to put away anything that will exalt itself against the knowledge of God to the obedience of Jesus Christ.

CHOOSE LIFE

CONCLUSION

FROM THE HEART OF THE AUTHOR

In conclusion, I hope and pray that this book has been a blessing to you. The goal of Messengers of Fire Ministries is to impact lives and to lead as many souls into the Kingdom of God as possible. My wife and I have made a commitment to lead souls into all truth – just as Jesus did for His people; in His physical ministry and is still doing with us today in the Spirit.

Saints, I would sincerely like for you to understand my heart and why I believe the Lord had me to write this book for you. It is not about me, but all about you; the believer in Messiah Jesus. From our hearts, I would truly like to thank you all for taking the time to read what the Holy Spirit desired for me to write in order to help catapult you into a triumphant life!

These truths that you have just read are faithful, and Love will be the foundation of our ministry into your hearts and minds for the rest of your life. This book was written solely to bring about transformation and peace in the Holy Spirit. It is not intended to hurt or condemn anyone, yet it was written in order to germinate throughout your spiritual walk with Christ for victorious living.

Janet and I would like to thank you all from the bottom of our hearts to yours for reading this book ... Messengers of Fire Ministries loves you all.

ABOUT THE AUTHOR

Born March 3, 1959 in Louisville, Kentucky, Dr. Theodore L. Dones is an apostolic revivalist. He is president and founder of Messengers of Fire Ministries. His ministry itinerates across the nation and crosses over denominational boundaries and geographical borders to fulfill what the Lord has called them to do: to stir up the churches, telling them to get ready for the coming revival.

Dr. Dones' greatest desire is this one thing: To be an instrument for God to, *"open the eyes of His people and turn them from darkness to light, from the power of satan to God so they may receive forgiveness of sins and inheritance among those who are sanctified by faith in Jesus Christ."* He has worked vigilantly, using every resource and opportunity that God sends his way to accomplish his call.

Apostle Ted Dones attended *International Circle of Faith College, Seminaries and Universities*, joining alumni such as Pastor Paula White, Bishop Noel Jones, attorney Julian McPhillips, Bishop Paul Morton and others.

He lays down his life to help leadership grow in foundational truths that must be established before works of faith are built upon them. He has helped thousands tear down the unproductive ways which seem right to a man and replaced them with the ways of the Lord. Ultimately, Dr. Dones will see his vision fulfilled that the Lord gave him several years ago. He will build a 2500-seat training center with an emphasis on the nine Gifts of the Spirit. The center will act as a resource hub for the Five Fold Ministry and believers will be dispersed back out into the world, fully equipped to make disciples.

The fruit of his international ministry has been in the works for more than fifteen years. Five Fold Connection (www.fivefoldconnection.com) is a leadership networking site equivalent to Facebook, which has recently launched and is connecting God's people with rapid results.

This site provides a God-rated environment for families to enjoy Godly conversations, posts, and teachings. Christian gaming and other enhancements are being added as well. The Messengers of Fire Bible College, which opened in 2011, affords everyone an opportunity to learn God's Word online: www.mofmchristianuniversity.org.

Dr. Ted Dones has reached nations for God on television (WBNA TV Channel 285) and radio, affecting many souls during his recent trip to Africa. His latest book titled, *Exposing Secrets of the Heart*, is greatly anticipated and will be released globally in the latter part of 2018.

Leadership conferences, weekly local church services and international ministry are just another part of Dr. Dones' everyday life. He relies fully on God's grace, presence and anointing, being fully aware of his personal inability to do anything good without Christ. He watches in amazement as God continually sends people into his life to support all aspects of the vision. He greatly anticipates the day when God's plan is complete and all the glory is given to Father God!

Dr. Dones is married to Janet, they have been married since 1980 and have one daughter and four grandchildren.

SCRIPTURE OUTLINE

Introduction
"The secrets of his heart will be revealed, and as a result he will fall facedown and worship God, proclaiming, "God is really among you." (1 Corinthians 14:25 CSB)

CHAPTER 1
"For where your treasure is, there will your heart be also. The light of the body is the eye: if therefore thine eye be single, thy whole body shall be full of light. But if thine eye be evil, thy whole body shall be full of darkness. If therefore the light that is in thee be darkness, how great is that darkness! No man can serve two masters: for either he will hate the one, and love the other; or else he will hold to the one, and despise the other. Ye cannot serve God and mammon." (Matthew 6:21-24)

"Their sentence is based on this fact: that the Light from heaven came into the world, but they loved the darkness more than the Light, for their deeds were evil. They hated the heavenly Light because they wanted to sin in the darkness. They turn away from that Light for fear their sins would be exposed and they would be punished. But those doing right came gladly to the Light to let everyone see that they were doing what God wants them to do." (John 3:19-21 TLB)

"Sin lurks deep in the hearts of the wicked, forever urging them on to evil deeds. They have no fear of God to hold them back. Instead, in their conceit, they think they can hide their evil deeds and not get caught. Everything they say is crooked and deceitful; they are no longer wise and good. They lie awake at night to hatch their evil plots, instead of planning how to keep away from wrong." (Psalm 36:1-4 TLB)

"This is the message which we have heard from Him and declare to you, that God is light, and in Him is no darkness at all. If we say that we have fellowship with Him, and walk in darkness, we lie, and do not practice the truth: But if we walk in the light as He is in the light, we have

fellowship with one another, and the blood of Jesus Christ His Son cleanses us from all sin." (1 John 1:5-7 NKJV)

"He who sins is of the devil, for the devil sinned from the beginning. For this purpose the Son of God was manifested, that He might destroy the works of the devil." (1 John 3:8 NKJV)

"Create in me a clean heart, O God, and renew a steadfast spirit within me. Do not cast me away from Your presence, and do not take Your Holy Spirit from me. Restore to me the joy of Your salvation, and uphold me with Your generous Spirit. Then I will teach transgressors Your ways, and sinners shall be converted to You." (Psalms 51:10-13 NKJV)

"Therefore, brothers, since we have confidence to enter the Most Holy Place by the blood of Jesus, By a new and living way opened for us through the curtain, that is, His body, And since we have a great priest over the house of God, Let us draw near to God with a sincere heart in full assurance of faith, having our hearts sprinkled to cleanse us from a guilty conscience and having our bodies washed with pure water." (Hebrews 10:19-22 NIV)

CHAPTER 2
"And they overcame him by the blood of the Lamb, and by the word of their testimony; and they loved not their lives unto the death." (Revelation 12:11)

"... broad is the way that leads to destruction, ... but narrow is the way that leads to life and few will find it." (Matthew 7:13-14 NKJV)

"But now, after that you have known God, or rather are known by God, how is it that you turn again to the weak and beggarly elements, to which you desire again to be in bondage?" (Galatians 4:9 NKJV, emphasis added.)

"Dear brothers, I have been talking to you as though you were still just babies in Christian life, who are not following the Lord, but your own desires; I cannot talk to you as I would to healthy Christians, who are filled with the Spirit. I have had to feed you with milk and not with solid food, because you couldn't digest anything stronger. And even now you still have to be fed with milk. For you are still only baby Christians, controlled by your own desires, not God's. When you are jealous of one another and divide up into quarreling groups, doesn't that prove you are still babies, wanting your own way? In fact, you are acting like people who do not belong to the Lord at all." (I Corinthians 3:1-3 TLB)

CHAPTER 3

"Not every one who says to Me, "Lord, Lord, shall enter the kingdom of heaven, but he who does the will of My Father in heaven. Many will say to Me in that day, Lord, Lord, have we not prophesied in Your name, cast out demons in Your name? And then I will declare to them, I never knew you; depart from Me, you that practice lawlessness!" (Matthew 7:21-23 NKJV)

"For God's gifts and His call are irrevocable. He never withdraws them when once they are given, and He does not change His mind about those to whom He gives His grace or to whom He sends His call." (Romans 11:29 AMP)

"And Jesus being full of the Holy Ghost returned from Jordan, and was led by the Spirit into the wilderness, Being forty days tempted of the devil. And in those days He did eat nothing: and when they were ended, He afterward hungered. And Jesus answered and said to him," It has been said, *"You shall not tempt the Lord your God. Now when the devil had ended every temptation, he departed from Him until an opportune time."* (Luke 4:1-2, 12-13 NKJV)

"When the devil had finished all this tempting, he left Him until an opportune time." (Luke 4:13 NIV)

"And if ye call on him as Father, who without respect of persons judgeth according to each man's work, pass the time of your sojourning in fear." (1 Peter 1:17 ASV)

"Not every one who says to Me, "Lord, Lord, shall enter the kingdom of heaven, but he who does the will of My Father in heaven. Many will say to Me in that day, Lord, Lord, have we not prophesied in Your name, cast out demons in Your name? And then I will declare to them, I never knew you; depart from Me, you that practice lawlessness!" (Matthew 7:21-23 NKJV)

"Now he who plants and he who waters are one, and each will one will receive his own reward according to his labor." (1 Corinthians 3:8 NKJV)

"I have fought the good fight, I have finished the course, I have kept the faith. Finally, there is laid up for me the crown of righteousness, which the Lord, the righteous Judge, will give to me on that Day, and not to me only, but also to all who have loved His appearing." (2 Timothy 4:7-8 ASV)

"Blessed is the man that endures temptation; for when he has been proved, he will receive the crown of life, which the Lord has promised to those who love him." (James 1:12 NKJV)

"But he who does the truth comes to the light, that his deeds may be clearly seen, that they have been done in God." (John 3:21 NKJV)

CHAPTER 4

"But God demonstrated His own love toward us, in that, while we were still sinners, Christ died for us." (Romans 5:8 NKJV)

"Much more then, being now justified by his blood, shall we be saved from the wrath of God through him." (Romans 5:9 ASV)

"For when we were still without strength, in due time Christ died for the ungodly. For scarcely for a righteous man will one die; yet perhaps for a good man someone would even dare to die. But God demonstrated His own love toward us, in that, while we were still sinners, Christ died for us." (Romans 5:6-8 NKJV)

"But God demonstrates his own love for us ... (when) Christ died for us." (Romans 5:8 NIV, word in parenthesis was added.)

"For God so loved the world, that he gave his only begotten Son, that whoever believes in Him should not perish, but have everlasting life. For God did not send His Son into the world to condemn the world, but that the world through Him might be saved. He who believes on Him is not condemned; but he who does not believe is condemned already, because he has not believed in the name of the only begotten Son of God." (John 3:16-18 NKJV)

"Or do you show contempt for the riches of his kindness, tolerance and patience, not realizing that God's kindness leads you toward repentance?" (Romans 2:4 NIV)
"Now hope does not disappoint, because the love of God has been poured out in our hearts by the Holy Ghost, who was given to us." (Romans 5:5 NKJV)

"Let us draw near with a true heart in full assurance of faith, having our hearts sprinkled from an evil conscience, and our bodies washed with pure water." (Hebrews 10:22 NKJV)

"But we all, with unveiled face, beholding as in a mirror the glory of the Lord, are being transformed into the same image from glory to glory, just as by the Spirit of the Lord."(2 Corinthians 3:18 NKJV)

"I have been crucified with Christ; it is no longer I who live, but Christ lives in me; and the life which I now live in the flesh I live by faith in the Son of God, who loved me and gave Himself for me." (Galatians 2:20 NKJV)

CHAPTER 5

"But as it is written: "Eye has not seen, nor ear heard, Nor have entered into the heart of man the things which God has prepared for those who love Him. But God has revealed them to us through His Spirit. For the Spirit searches all things, yes, the deep things of God."(I Corinthians 2:9-10 NKJV)

"But as it is written: "Eye has not seen, nor ear heard, Nor have entered into the heart of man the things which God has prepared for those who love Him. But God has revealed them to us through His Spirit. For the Spirit searches all things, yes, the deep things of God. For what man knows the things of a man except the spirit of the man which is in him? Even so no one knows the things of God except the Spirit of God. Now we have received, not the spirit of the world, but the Spirit who is from God, that we might know the things that have been freely given to us by God."(I Corinthians 2:9-12 NKJV)

"In the beginning was the Word, and the Word was with God, and the Word was God. He was in the beginning with God. All things were made by Him, and without Him nothing was made that was made. In Him was life, and the life was the light of men. And the light shines in darkness and the darkness did not comprehend it."(John 1:1-5 NKJV)

CHAPTER 6

"As His divine power has given to us all things that pertain to life and godliness, through the knowledge of Him who called us by glory and virtue: By which have been given to us exceedingly great and precious promises, that through these you may be partakers of the divine nature, having escaped the corruption that is in the world through lust."(II Peter 1:3-4 NKJV)

"Though I speak with the tongues of men and of angels, but have not love, I have become as sounding brass or a clanging cymbal. And though I have the gift of prophecy, and understand all mysteries and all knowledge, and though I have all faith, so that I could remove

mountains, but have not love, I am nothing. And though I bestow all my goods to feed the poor, and though I give my body to be burned, but have not love, it profits me nothing. "(1 Corinthians 13:1-3 NKJV)

"Now see that I, even I, am He, and there is no God besides Me: I kill and I make alive; I wound, and I heal: nor is there any who can deliver out from My hand." (Deuteronomy 32:39 NKJV)

"For the law of the Spirit of life in Christ Jesus has made me free from the law of sin and death. For what the law could not do in that it was weak through the flesh, God did by sending His own Son in the likeness of sinful flesh, on account of sin: He condemned sin in the flesh, That the righteous requirement of the law might be fulfilled in us who do not walk according to the flesh, but according to the Spirit." (Romans 8:2-4 NKJV)

"As His divine power has given to us all things that pertain to life and godliness, through the knowledge of Him who called us by glory and virtue: By which have been given to us exceedingly great and precious promises, that through these you may be partakers of the divine nature, having escaped the corruption that is in the world through lust." (II Peter 1:3-4 NKJV)

CHAPTER 7

"But God demonstrates His own love toward us, in that while we were still sinners, Christ died for us. Much more then, having now been justified by His blood, we shall be saved from wrath through Him." (Romans 5:8-9 NIV)

"Therefore put to death your members which are upon the earth: fornication, uncleanness, passion, evil desire, and covetousness, which is idolatry." (Colossians 3:5 NKJV)

"For we have spent enough of our past lifetime in doing the will of the Gentiles-when we walked in licentiousness, lusts, drunkenness, revelries, drinking parties, and abominable idolatries." (I Peter 4:3 NKJV)

"Because of these things the wrath of God is coming on the children of disobedience." (Colossians 3:6 NKJV)

"What if God, wanting to show His wrath and to make His power known, endured with much longsuffering the vessels of wrath fitted to destruction: And that He might make known the riches of His glory on the vessels of mercy, which He had beforehand prepared unto glory." (Romans 9: 22-23 NKJV)

"To them God willed to make known what are the riches of the glory of this mystery among the Gentiles: which is Christ in you, the hope of glory. Him we preach, warning every man, and teaching every man in all wisdom, that we may present every man perfect, in Christ Jesus." (Colossians 1:27-28 NKJV)

"That He might sanctify and cleanse it with the washing of water by the Word, That He might present it to Himself a glorious church, not having spot, or wrinkle, or any such thing; but that it should be holy and without blemish." (Ephesians 5:26-27 NKJV)

"In the first year of his reign, in the first month, he opened the doors of the house of the Lord, and repaired them. Then he brought in the priests and the Levites, and gathered them together in the East Square, And said unto them: "Hear me, you Levites! Now sanctify yourselves, sanctify the house of the Lord God of your fathers, and carry forth the rubbish from the holy place. For our fathers have trespassed and done evil in the eyes of the Lord our God; they have forsaken Him, have turned their faces away from the habitation of the Lord, and turned their backs on Him. They have also shut up the doors of the vestibule, put out the lamps, and have not burned incense or offered burnt offerings in the Holy Place to the God of Israel. Therefore the wrath of the Lord fell upon Judah and Jerusalem, and He has given them up to trouble, to astonishment, and to jeering, as you see with your eyes." (II Chronicles 29:3-8 NKJV, emphasis added.)

"Do you not know that you are the temple of God, and that the Spirit of God dwells in you? If anyone defile the temple of God, God will destroy him. For the temple of God is holy, which temple you are." (1 Corinthians 3:16-17 NKJV)

"Do you not discern and understand that you [the whole church at Corinth] are God's temple (His sanctuary), and that God's Spirit has His permanent dwelling in you [to be at home in you] collectively as a church and also individually?" (1 Corinthians 6:19 AMP)

"Cleanse your hands and purify your hearts and God will draw nigh to you." (James 4:8 KJV)

"How can a young man cleanse his way? By taking heed according to Your word. With my whole heart I have sought You; Oh, let me not wander from Your commandments! Your word I have hidden in mine

heart, That I might not sin against You. Blessed art You, O Lord! Teach me Your statutes."(Psalm 119:9-12 NKJV)

"But what things were gain to me, these I counted loss for Christ. But indeed I also count all things loss for the excellence of the knowledge of Christ Jesus my Lord, for whom I have suffered the loss of all things, and count them as rubbish, that I may gain Christ, And be found in Him, not having my own righteousness, which is from the law, but that which is through faith in Christ, the righteousness which is from God by faith; That I may know Him and the power of his resurrection, and the fellowship of his sufferings, being conformed to His death. If, by any means, I might attain to the resurrection of the dead."(Philippians 3:7-11 NKJV)

CHAPTER 8
"When He had called the people unto Him, with His disciples also, He said to them, "Whoever desires to come after Me, let him deny himself, and take up his cross, and follow Me. For whoever desires to save his life will lose it, but whoever loses his life for My sake and the gospel's, will save it. For what will it profit a man if he gains the whole world, and loses his own soul? Or what shall a man give in exchange for his soul?"(Mark 8:34-37 NKJV)

"Do not be deceived, God is not mocked; for whatever a man sows that he will also reap. For he who sows to his flesh will of the flesh reap corruption, but he who sows to the Spirit will of the Spirit reap everlasting life."(Galatians 6:7-8 NKJV)

CHAPTER 9
"For I through the law died to the law, that I might live to God." (Galatians 2:19 NKJV)

"that the righteousness requirement of the law might be fulfilled in us, who do not walk according to the flesh, but according to the Spirit." (Romans 8:4 NKJV)

"O foolish Galatians! Who has bewitched you, that you should not obey the truth, before whose eyes Jesus Christ was clearly portrayed among you as crucified? This only I want to learn from you: Did you receive the Spirit by the works of the law, or by the hearing of faith? Are you so foolish? Having begun in the Spirit, are you now being made perfect by the flesh?(Galatians 3:1- 3 NKJV)

"Knowing that a man is not justified by the works of the law, but by the faith of Jesus Christ, even we have believed in Jesus Christ, that we might be justified by the faith of Christ, and not by the works of the law: for by the works of the law shall no flesh be justified. But if, while we seek to be justified by Christ, we ourselves also are found sinners, is therefore Christ the minister of sin? God forbid. For if I build again the things which I destroyed, I make myself a transgressor."(Galatians 2:16-18)

"I say then: Walk in the Spirit, and you shall not fulfill the lust of the flesh. But if you are led of the Spirit, you are not under the law. And those who are Christ's have crucified the flesh with its passions and desires. If we live in the Spirit, let us also walk in the Spirit."(Galatians 5:16, 18, 24, 25 NKJV)

"Now the works of the flesh are evident, which are: adultery, fornication, uncleanness, licentiousness, idolatry, sorcery, hatred, contentions, jealousies, outbursts of wrath, selfish ambitions, dissensions, heresies, envy, murders, drunkenness, revelries, and the like; of the which, I tell you beforehand, just as I also told you in time past, that those who practice such things will not inherit the kingdom of God."(Galatians 5:19-21 NKJV)

"But the fruit of the Spirit is love, joy, peace, longsuffering, kindness, goodness, faithfulness, gentleness, self-control. Against such there is no law."(Galatians 5:22-23 NKJV)

CHAPTER 10
"But the fruit of the Spirit is love, joy, peace, longsuffering, kindness, goodness, faithfulness, gentleness, self-control. Against such there is no law."(Galatians 5:222-23 NKJV)

"And those who are Christ's have crucified the flesh with its passions and desires."(Galatians 5:24 NKJV)

"For you are still carnal. For where there are envy, strife, and divisions, among you are you not carnal and behaving like mere men?" (1 Corinthians 3:3 NKJV)

"I press toward the goal for the prize of the upward call of God in Christ Jesus. Therefore let us, as many as are mature, having this mind; and if in any thing you think otherwise, God will reveal even this to you. Nevertheless, to the degree that we have already attained, let us walk by the same rule, let us be of the same mind. Brethren, join in the following

my example, and note those who so walk, as you have us for a pattern." (Philippians 3:14-17 NKJV)

"Therefore be imitators of God [copy Him and follow His example, as well-beloved children imitate their father]." (Ephesians 5:1 AMP)

"Therefore having these promises, beloved, let us cleanse ourselves from all filthiness of the flesh and spirit, perfecting holiness in the fear of God." (II Corinthians 7:1 NKJV)
"For the law made nothing perfect; on the other hand, there is bringing in of a better hope, through which we draw near to God." (Hebrews 7:19 NKJV)

CHAPTER 11
"But let patience have her perfect work, that you may be perfect and complete, lacking nothing." (James 1:4 NKJV)

"Now may the God of peace, who brought up our Lord Jesus from the dead, that great Shepherd of the sheep, through the blood of the everlasting covenant, make you complete in every good work to do His will, working in you what is well pleasing in his sight, through Jesus Christ; to whom be glory for ever and ever. Amen." (Hebrews 13:20-21 NKJV)

"For we are glad, when we are weak, and you are strong. And this also we pray that you may be made complete." (II Corinthians 13:9 NKJV)

"My brethren, count it all joy when you fall into various trials." (James 1:2 NKJV)

"But let patience have her perfect work, that you may be perfect and complete, lacking nothing." (James 1:4 NKJV)

"Therefore having these promises, beloved, let us cleanse ourselves from all filthiness of the flesh and spirit, perfecting holiness in the fear of God." (II Corinthians 7:1 NKJV)

"But the fruit of the Spirit is love, joy, peace, longsuffering, kindness, goodness, faithfulness, Gentleness, self-control. Against such there is no law." (Galatians 5:22-23 NKJV)

CHAPTER 12

"For the wrath of God is revealed from heaven against all ungodliness and unrighteousness of men, who hold the truth in unrighteousness." (Romans 1:18 NKJV)

"For God did not appoint us to wrath, but to obtain salvation through our Lord Jesus Christ." (1 Thessalonians 5:9 NKJV)

"Beware lest anyone cheat you through philosophy and empty deceit, according to the tradition of men, according to the basic principles of the world, and not according to Christ. For in Him dwells all the fullness of the Godhead bodily; and you are complete in Him, who is the head of all principality and power." (Colossians 2:8-10 NKJV)

"Resist the devil and he will flee from you." (James 4:7)

"And Adam lived one hundred and thirty years, and begot a son in his own likeness, after his image; and called his name Seth." (Genesis 5:3 NKJV, emphasis added.)

"Because of unbelief they could not enter into His rest." (Hebrews 3:11 NKJV)

"And my God shall supply all your need according to His riches in glory by Christ Jesus." (Philippians 4:19, emphasis added.)

"For the Lord God is a sun and shield; the Lord will give grace and glory; no good thing will He withhold from those who walk uprightly." (Psalms 84:11 NKJV)

"And you shall know the truth, and the truth shall set you free." (John 8:32)

"For to be carnally minded is death, but to be spiritually minded is life and peace. Because the carnal mind is enmity [hostile, hatred] against God: for it is not subject to the law of God, nor indeed can be." (Romans 8:6-8 NKJV)

"We have all sinned and fallen short of the glory of God." (Romans 3:23 NKJV)

"But the hour is coming, and now is, when the true worshipers will worship the Father in spirit and truth; for the Father is seeking such to worship Him. God is Spirit, and those who worship Him must worship in spirit and truth." (John 4:22, 23 NKJV)

"I tell you that if these should keep silent, the stones would immediately cry out."(Luke 19:40 NKJV)

"But if you be led of the Spirit, you are not under the law."(Galatians 5:18 NKJV)

"that He might present it to Himself a glorious church, not having spot or wrinkle or any such thing, but that it should be holy and without blemish."(Ephesians 5:27)

"Let him turn away from evil and do good; let him seek peace and pursue it. For the eyes to the Lord are on the righteous, and His ears are open to their prayers: but the face of the Lord is against those who do evil." (I Peter 3:11, 12 NKJV)

"And then I will declare to them, "I never knew you; depart from Me, you who practice lawlessness!"(Matthew 7:23 NKJV)

For all that is in the world-the lust of the flesh, the lust of the eyes and the pride of life-is not of the Father, but is of the world."(I John 2:16)

"I can do all things through Christ who strengthens me."(Philippians 4:13 NKJV)

ENDNOTES

Chapter 1

1. In the Greek, we find the words *kroop-tos* and *kroop-to* which mean, "*concealed [by covering]; hide.*"[1]

2. The Hebrew word is *tah-al-oom-maw* and it means, "Thing that is hid; to veil from sight or conceal."[2]

3. In Webster's dictionary, the word *overpower* means "*to overcome by superior force; to defeat.*"[3]

4. The word *overcome* in the Greek language is *nikao¯*, pronounced as *nik-as-o*–meaning "*to conquer, subdue, prevail, and get victory.*"[4]

5. In the Hebrew language, the word *overcome* is *yaˆkoˆl*, pronounced yaw-kole–meaning "*to be able, attain, endure, and have power.*"[5]

Chapter 2

6. The word *element* in the Greek language is *stoykhion*–meaning "*basic fundamental principles.*"[6]

Chapter 7

7. Frangipane made the following statement in his book: "*Within every Christian there is a secret place, a sanctuary that we must prepare for the Lord. (You are that sanctuary.) This holy place is unlike the Holy of Holies in Jewish temples. Not until this place is clean will the Lord dwell in us in the fullness of His Spirit.*"[7]

Chapter 11

8. The word *entire* in the Greek language is *holokleros*–meaning "*complete, sound in every part.*"[8]

9. This word is synonymous with the Greek word *teleioteros* or *perfect*, indicating the development of every grace into maturity.[9]

APPENDIX A

Romans 10:9, 10

"... that if you confess with your mouth the Lord Jesus and believe in your heart that God has raised Him from the dead, you will be saved. For with the heart one believes unto righteousness, and with the mouth confession is made unto salvation."

Acts 2:21

"... And it shall come to pass that whoever calls on the name of the LORD Shall be saved."

www.ingramcontent.com/pod-product-compliance
Lightning Source LLC
Chambersburg PA
CBHW051909090426
42811CB00003B/514